LIFE BEYOND THE KEYHOLE

Chasity,
Thank you for your
support.
Best wishes,
Shena Koebel
AKA C. Sparks-

LIFE BEYOND THE KEYHOLE

C. SPARKS

SBPC

SIMMS BOOKS PUBLISHING CORPORATION

SBPC

SIMMS BOOKS PUBLISHING CORP.

Publishers Since 2012

Published by Simms Books Publishing Corporation

Jonesboro, GA

Library of Congress Cataloging in Publication Data

2020952335

LIFE BEYOND THE KEYHꝊLE

ISBN: 978-1-949433-16-6

Printed in the United States of America

Book Arrangement by Simms Books Publishing

Editor Mary Hoekstra

Cover by Chester Hopper

ACKNOWLEDGMENTS

I would like to acknowledge all those who told me I was ugly, stupid, and worthless, all those who told me I would never amount to anything, and all those who felt the need to mentally or physically abuse me. A big shout out to those who doubted me and didn't want to help me. If you were betting against me, you might want to get a refund.

DEDICATION

I want to dedicate this book to those who gave me a chance. To the few who believed in me when I doubted myself, Paul Lawson, my best friend for over 30 years, you never left my side and moved me more times than I can remember. Your strength, kindness, loyalty, and love have gotten me through some of my darkest times. Thank you and I love you.

My Aunt Sue and Uncle Roger, what a journey it has been. In my younger years, I was a handful and I am forever grateful that you took on the challenge of trying to raise me. I apologize that I did not make it easy, and again, even though we struggled, you never left me. You have always helped me when you could and now, as an adult, I realize how hard it must have been for you and I appreciate that you never gave up. I am sorry for putting you through so much in my younger years and I am blessed to still be a part of your family. Thank you and I love you.

My bosses and co-workers: I won't go into great detail but over the 15 years here, we have become a family. Thank you for seeing the change in me, knowing that something had to be done, and getting together to remove me from a very toxic situation. I truly feel that you all saved my life. Thank you, and yes, I love you all, too.

Dan Bergman, my co-worker, and friend of over 22 years. Thank you doesn't seem like enough to say but, I will scream it. THANK YOU! Your friendship and generosity will never be forgotten.

My husband, Karl, I have a page at the end of this book that tells you how grateful I am for you. Here, the short version is, I love you with my entire being. Your patience and love pulled me out of a very dark place, and I can never repay you for that. Thank you and I love you.

You accepted my flaws and all. It is because of you all that I am still here making things happen. I will never be the CEO of a large corporation or President of the US, but I'm living a good life, I've got everything I need and nothing that I don't.

With you all by my side, I found the courage, the strength, and the will to keep on moving. It was a slow pace, but at no point did I give up. I love you all; you played a part in my life and I will never forget you.

I hope life treats you kindly and that you achieve your goals.
Remember: A goal without a plan is just a dream!

Much Love,
C. Sparks

INTRODUCTION

In the end, you will meet three types of people: Those who are here for a SEASON; those who are here for a REASON; and those who are here for a LIFETIME.

All three types of people are important to you on your journey, so never regret crossing paths with any of them. Always appreciate those who told you NO! It's because of them that you learned to just do it yourself. You will eventually learn that some friendships are written in the stars, while others are written in the sand.

It's hard to come into the world and be all alone, with no father but with a mother who gave you up at the age of five. Some people say, "Walk a mile in my shoes, bet you couldn't do it!"

I just laugh and say, "Spend five minutes in my head, bet you couldn't do it!"

I've made it this far because I learned at a very young age to bury bad thoughts, to take myself to "another place," and to use humor to get me through. Some people have skeletons in their closet, NOT ME! I have a whole cemetery in the backyard, and I'm not afraid to dig them up one-by-one, sit down with them, and enjoy a cup of coffee while discussing old times.

I was asked, "What do you plan to achieve by writing this book?"
I responded, "This book is not meant to make you cry, nor is it meant to make you feel sorry for me. This book also is not here to trash people in my life and make me out to be a perfect angel."

We are not going to talk about me breaking my shoulder doing a cartwheel, or about that one time at band camp. This is not a journal of my every move. This book is meant to be uplifting and to let you know that you are not alone. I want to share that we are all entitled to our "choices," we are also equally entitled to the consequences of those choices.

We will laugh in this book; I laughed as I wrote it, you'll laugh as you read it. But there will be laughter along with feeling sad at times. When you are done with this book, it is my hope that you feel inspired and have a better understanding of why I am like I am, and how we can work together to help you get through this crazy journey called LIFE. YOU ARE NOT ALONE!

Yes, there's some therapy with writing this book, but also, I want to take a portion of my book sales to help kids in our community. Not sure what it will be yet, just know I want it to be a place where kids can just be kids.

"I want to make sure you all know: Your current situation is NOT your final destination. I'll say it a little louder for those of you in the back: YOUR CURRENT SITUATION IS NOT YOUR FINAL DESTINATION."

Each day you wake up on "this side" of the dirt, it's another opportunity to make a change. Look at it as another experience in your life. So many people won't wake tomorrow for the experience, so be grateful. The most important thing I want to tell you is, don't let outside noise drown out your inner peace.

So, let's do this! Grab your beverage of choice, slip off those shoes, put on some comfy socks, and if you're wearing a bra, feel free to let the girls out, and relax. Read a few pages, or read the whole book today. Either way, I want you to take one thing away from this reading experience and it is: Life is a journey. You will have flat tires, leaky radiators, snowstorms, icy roads, detours, roadblocks, and speed bumps. You will cross paths with so many different types of people along your journey. Some may be hitchhikers and some may just wave as you pass by each other on the road. Be kind. You never know when your car could break down and you're walking alone with your thumb out and just praying for someone to stop and help you.

Christmas Carol

– Skip Ewing

(my favorite Christmas song replace Christmas Carol with Little Sheila)

I was playin Santa Claus downtown on Christmas Eve
When a little girl of three or four climbed up onto my knee
I could tell she had a Christmas Wish behind those eyes of blue
So, I asked her what's your name, and what can Santa git for you
She said my name is Christmas Carol, I was born on Christmas Day
I don't know who my daddy is, and mommy's gone away
All I want for Christmas is someone to take me home

Does anybody want a Christmas Carol of their own?

We'll all I could say was "Santa will do the best he could"

And I set her down and told her "now to remember to be good"

She said I will then be walked away, turned and waved goodbye

And I'm glad she wasn't close enough to see ole Santa Cry

She said my name is Christmas Carol, I was born on Christmas Day

I don't know who my daddy is, and mommy's gone away

All I want for Christmas is someone to take me home

Does anybody want a Christmas Carol of their own?

Early Christmas morning I got up and dialed the phone

I made a few arrangements at the County Children's home

And they told me it would be alright to pick her up today

Now my little Christmas Carol won't ever have to say

My name is Christmas Carol, I was born on Christmas Day

I don't know who my daddy is, and mommy's gone away

All I want for Christmas is someone to take me home

Does anybody want a Christmas Carol of their own?

Chapter 1
"My Genesis"

If you asked anyone, "Do you remember being born?", most would say that they do not, it's only from their earliest recollection that they could remember. Naturally, no one ever really remembers the moment that they were born; making their way through the birth canal was for sure a messy and tight squeeze. Trust me when I say this, it won't be your last messy and tight squeeze. It gets worse as you get older.

Thinking back, my memories started at the age of four. I was born in Cook County, Illinois in 1964, smack dab in the middle of racial unrest, riots, a war, and new laws being passed on segregation.

During those early years, I had no clue what was going on around me and all the struggles that my mother was going through during those tough and difficult times.

I mentioned her going through some tough times and I'll explain to bring you up to speed. From what I remember, at age four, the year is 1968, the President of the United States of America is being blamed for the deadliest war to date. The country is being torn apart from racism, the peacemakers were assassinated, both Martin Luther King, Jr. and Robert F. Kennedy. There are riots and protests over the war and racial inequality, police brutality, people being killed, and people being denied rights because of the color of their skin.

Now catching you up, my mother and I were living in an apartment in Chicago, and the majority of the neighborhood was "colored people," as they were referred to back then. Bill, who I think was my mom's boyfriend, (she had me call him Dad) was "colored" also. It was later determined he was not my dad, but he and a little girl named Charlotte, whom I think was his daughter, were around sometimes. They came and went; I don't know if we lived with them or if they lived with us.

In my neighborhood, I stuck out like a sore thumb. I was a little, pale, white girl with long blonde hair past my butt, and I was surrounded by what I was always told were, "colored people."

I remember that we lived across the street from the hospital. How do I remember this? Because I remember watching my mother walk across the street many times to get help after Bill would beat her up. They would always have arguments that led to fights and my mother being beaten up and badly bruised and bleeding.

Looking on the brighter side of things, Bill never did anything to me or Charlotte. He would just yell at me and her, but never once did he put his hands on us. I remember thinking, *When I grow up, I don't want a man named Bill as my husband. Bills are mean and scary.*

He was always abusing my mother. I remember him calling her horrible names and threatening to kill her.

I remember all those fights that they had, and for some reason, it seemed like he had a lot of hate for my mom. I remember her crying herself to sleep, while I slept out on the couch. I knew that my mom loved Bill.

When they were not fighting, she would dance around the apartment with a hairbrush in her hand singing, "Marry me, Bill," to a song called *Wedding Bell Blues* by the Fifth Dimension. She was a different person when she turned this song up loud and sang along. She smiled and she was so beautiful, even with black eyes and swollen lips.

That was my mother's burden, being in love with a black man during the most volatile time in our country's history, and especially during a time when it was not acceptable.

Those fights between my mom and Bill frightened me, but afterward, I found some kind of comfort; it was my mother's antics. I didn't know if she was doing it to cover up what just happened by being silly and singing along to the music to help me cope.

3

I don't have the answers, but for some strange reason, it helped me cope. I would find myself wandering off, putting on music to calm my nerves, and even trying to imitate her dancing around singing, or just playing a tune in my head. That seemed the best way to escape what was going on in her world, and I accepted it, unconsciously, in mine.

My mom did not raise me to be afraid of people because of the color of their skin, she actually wanted me to embrace it. Her telling me that Bill was my father would have made Charlotte my sister. I didn't have a hate for him or her, or even the kids I met outside in the streets, or the ones who did Double-Dutch in the parking lot.

The trauma that we went through as babies made me make up in my mind that the person that Bill was, and how he treated my mother, made me not want a man like Bill.

When it was good, it was good, meaning the times that they were not fighting were good times, too few to count, but I do remember those good times.

It seemed like music was the common thread to solving life's issues and dramas. I know for sure it helped my mom cope. Being that we were in a predominately black neighborhood, that's all we would hear, some rhythm and blues-type songs. I was young, so I could not classify what type of music it was, but it was music that we heard playing all the time. Before we went to bed and even long into the night, somebody was playing music.

I remember looking out the window and seeing the police pull up and harass some of the people in the street because the music was playing too loud. It became almost like a buffer for me also; whenever they would fight, I would go to the stereo and turn the music up, hoping that once they heard the music it would have them come out happy, singing to one another.

Chapter 2
"Innocence"

Among other ways of coping, I found my surroundings helped me deal with a lot of those horrible times. I would escape during the day, going down the three flights of stairs to play in the parking lot with the other little girls. They taught me a jump rope game called Double-Dutch. Yes! I was just as good at Double-Dutch as they were, and they were a little shocked by that.

I didn't get to play with these girls often because I was normally locked in the apartment. Most of the time I was alone, or it was me and Charlotte by ourselves. It was always an adventure that I welcomed, not only learning Double-Dutch jump rope but making new friends and building a bond. I learned a lot about them, and even though I was different than them, they were very curious about getting to know me.

I remember seeing the police coming around one day and them ushering me off to the side of the parking lot. They were very concerned. I could pick up from the sound of their voices and the looks on their faces that something was wrong. I didn't know it then, but later on in life, I would understand that the relationship between "coloreds" and police was not a great one at all.

I hadn't experienced mistreatment because of the color of my skin at that point, and it bothered me. I could understand, at that young age, that it was a problem and it caused great fear in the girls I considered friends doing Double-Dutch jump rope in the middle of the parking lot.

My mother stayed on the go, so the times that I could sneak away to go play Double-Dutch, I really took a chance getting caught by her and getting into big trouble. Most times, I listened to her, because knowing what I knew about the things that were going on in the streets, it was in my best interest to just stay inside and keep the doors locked.

I enjoyed having interaction with other people outside of my apartment, I was so closed in, and the only other person I spoke to was Charlotte. She was younger than me, so I was left with the responsibility to look after her from time to time, and to be honest, she wasn't my favorite person.

For a time in my life, I felt like Cinderella; at times, my mother could be the evil stepmother or the fairy godmother, it just depended on the day. Charlotte was for sure the little stepsister who was treated differently and enjoyed all the things that I wanted out of life.

I hated Christmas. To this day, Christmas is my least favorite holiday. I remember one year for Christmas all I wanted was a *Farmer SEE N' SAY*. That's all I asked for, but I didn't get one; Charlotte did and she wouldn't share it. She would hide it when she wasn't playing with it. All I got was a doll and I know some of you think I was an ungrateful kid. NO! I wasn't. I just wanted one gift, not five gifts, not ten gifts, just one gift! But she got a bunch of gifts and one of those gifts was what I wanted so bad.

Charlotte got everything that I wanted. I'm not going to "sugarcoat" a dog turd and roll it in sprinkles and try to sell it to you as an Amish cookie. I did not like her! I would sleep on one couch at night and she would sleep on the smaller couch. I used to wet the couch, so I would get up and move her over there to make it look like she wet the couch. Why? Because I wanted her to get in trouble. She was always treated better, so any chance I had, I tried to get her in trouble, but it always backfired on me.

One time, we were left alone; I was five she was four. We got into the kitchen cabinets and got out all the oatmeal, sugar and flour, and anything else we could find that would make the floor slippery. We poured it all out on the floor. I should say, "Charlotte poured it out," I just got it out of the cabinet for her. Then we ran and slid on the slippery floor and we'd be covered in flour and oatmeal and laughing so loud. It was so much fun!

That same day, I looked in the fridge and saw some chocolate wrapped in tin foil, and I thought it was a new candy bar. I loved Mr. Goodbars™, but this didn't look like a Mr. Goodbar™, but I figured it was chocolate so it would do. I broke the bar up, sharing it with Charlotte. I got the bigger piece, being the oldest, and she got the smaller piece.

A little while later, we were both in the bathroom, pooping. It wasn't chocolate. It was Ex-Lax™! We were so sick. My mother was so mad at us. But as usual, I got in more trouble than Charlotte did because I was always the bad influence. I was the oldest and I should have known better.

Life was hard and I knew something was going on; my mom spent a lot of time away. I later learned she was out prostituting and stealing stuff. We spent a lot of time alone; I was always told that I was "in charge" and to watch Charlotte and keep her safe. And I always thought that was odd. Who was going to watch me and keep me safe?

I grew up fast and I learned, at a very young age, to cook and do dishes while standing on a chair. We didn't have much, but what we did have, I was supposed to keep up.

One thing I hated was the cockroaches! Those things were huge! I was scared of them; I could hear them at night. I would turn on the light and they would scatter. They were so big, and even though I was told they wouldn't hurt me, I still was not comfortable with them. Charlotte named a couple of them and considered them pets. NOT ME!... I didn't want anything to do with those creepy creatures!

Every so often, a guy would show up to help us get rid of them. I thought he was sucking them up with the little contraption he brought with him, and I was always scared he might accidentally suck me up in the machine, so I would jump onto my mom's bed and mentally take myself to a different place. I would stare at the ceiling and rip up little pieces of white toilet paper, and I would pretend like I was at the movie theater watching a Mickey Mouse movie and eating popcorn.

I had the ability to always take myself "somewhere else" to cope. That really helped me. I could imagine those big, creepy cockroaches trying to eat me. My worst fear was that a whole family of them would get on me and devour me! I woke up in a cold sweat, jumping out of my sleep right before the killer roaches could eat me.

That night, I walked over to the stereo set and pushed play on the cassette, and out came the sounds of water and a voice singing. As I sat there listening, I could follow the singer talking about sitting and waiting on things to change. In my little mind, I felt I was doing the same, waiting for things to change; not being the overseer of a little brat, having so many rules, when all I wanted to do was go outside and play with my friends and just be a kid.

As I stared out the window listening to the song, the singer had taken a trip far away from his home and later wound up right back in the same spot. I always wondered if he actually took the trip, or in his mind, he had traveled there, kind of like what I did when I had enough of what was going on around me and wished I was somewhere else.

I fell in love with that song for the "what ifs," just being able to travel out of my life and see the world, but I worried that I would only see it in my dreams and still be just like him, waiting and watching as the tide rolled away.

I heard footsteps coming down the hall so I hurried up, turned off the cassette player, and jumped back on my couch. My mom came into the living room.

"Who was playing that music?"

She came over to me and nestled down close to me on the couch, rubbing my back and playing with my hair.

"Yes, Little Sheila, I felt the same way, that's why I left and tried to make something of myself," she whispered in my ear. Then she kissed me and went back into the bedroom.

That night I dreamt of so many things. I had a great imagination. I thought about that song, and as much as I loved the song, I didn't want to just wind up back where I started. I jumped on a boat and told the captain I was going on a trip and did not want to come back to that dock. Take me anywhere, but here!

"Hurry, hurry! We don't have time! Sail away Captain! Sail away!" Off we went on a cruise around the world, me and my mom. Charlotte and Bill were left at the docks and that was just fine with me.

I imagined my mom's smiling face as we both held hairbrush handles, singing to one another as the wind blew through our hair, and the captain chartered a course for "Anywhere but Here."

Each night that week was an adventure and the score of our newly found zeal for this adventure was nothing short of amazing!

I must have played the radio and all of my mom's cassettes more than three times apiece. Most of the time I was by myself, as Bill and Charlotte would come and go, but I made the best of that week, and I remember seeing my mother happy.

There was one song I found that was not like the other songs I would hear on the radio, or even in her cassette collection. Again, I was very aware and listened to the words of the song that gave me inspiration and helped me through the times when I was alone. It had become a conversation and the music spoke to me. It was more of the same music, in a sense, telling me to explore the world, get ready and see the wonderful, big world. The chorus had me! I would scream, "Born to be wild!" running and dancing around the apartment.

My friends, my Double-Dutch buddies, had not heard the best song known to man, so I had to share it with them. One day, after my mother gave me her safety instructions, I snuck out and asked a couple of friends if they had heard this new song that I kept repeating over and over again. They all started singing it with me. They had not heard it at all, judging from their reactions, but they were amused and followed right along as I pumped my fist and did my best to remember the first lines of lyrics from memory, so I stuck to the chorus. I had a blast that day, out of the house, Double-Dutching against my mother's wishes, and singing a song that stated I was free and born to be wild.

I knew I was on the verge of really getting in trouble so I cut my adventure short that day and hurried into the apartment before my mother got back. I spent the rest of the day waiting for that song to come back on. I guess by accident I found the WLS station in Chicago that played that song later that night, and I had a ball dancing around and yelling at the top of my lungs again, "Born to be wild!"

Chapter 3
"Waiting Patiently"

Yes, I can say that my young life was not peaches and cream, or a walk in the park by any stretch of the imagination. We had good days and bad ones. I was a latchkey kid, so I was made to feel like a grown person when I was only a baby.

My mom always told me, "You're a big girl," or, "You are in charge," or, "It's your responsibility..." Now, for a little kid, those are very big shoes to fill. I got used to my mother barking orders to me, making me feel like it all fell on my little shoulders. Lil Sheila was actually Big Sheila at all other times in my life, but only till bedtime, when I was tucked in sometimes.

You would think this was too much for a little girl to take on, but for those of you who grew up just like me, you understand fully how it felt, and even when you heard these glorious words. Being used to being told what to do 24/7, and then one day, you're asked....

"What would you like?"

"Huh? What?! You asking me? Me?"

It is like God opened the Heavens and came down HIMSELF and asked you, "What would you like, My child?"

Let me do my best to explain the feeling, because God's honest truth, I had only felt this way one other time in my life, when that question did not feel laborious; it was pure freedom to say what I wanted, and it was going to be given unto me.

I had been made to endure so much as a child, from watching my mom being abused, feeling alone, and knowing that I was defenseless, my words and requests had gone upspoken in fear of any type of backlash. And I had finally been summoned...

At that very moment, I felt closer to my mother than I had ever felt; she was mine again, I didn't have to share her with anyone else in the world. No sharing her with Bill, Charlotte, the streets, her addiction, her fears... it was just us.

My heart exploded with pure joy at that moment that she would trust in me to make a decision so salient to the planning of her going to the corner store.

She stated she was going to the corner store and asked me:

"What do you want?"

This was one of the most memorable moments in my life. I reveled, I celebrated, I rejoiced in that question, getting my response together. I had to take a deep breath. Between the excitement and giggles, I was able to blurt out my request.

"Yes," I yelled! "I want a Mr. Goodbar™!"

When I was good, that was my treat of choice, that thick chocolate bar with lots of peanuts (not the way they are today). I loved candy, but that was Number One on my list. Now, being able to verbalize it in the form of a request...Whew! I was in heaven.

My Mom said she would be back shortly; she had to get some milk, a camera, and yes, she would get me a Mr. Goodbar™. I could hardly wait for her to come back.

As usual, I was told to lock the door behind her, which was a screwdriver that we stuck through the latch. And I knew the rules: Do not answer the door for anybody. She would be back shortly.

I waited and I waited and, well, waited some more. I so wanted my candy bar. It had started to get dark. I had played all her cassettes again and listened to the radio. I sat and looked out the window at all the ambulances going to the hospital. I was getting worried, because the streetlights were coming on and she wasn't back.

Daylight turned to night and I eventually fell asleep on the couch. I was alone and not really scared, but I remember feeling very alone, hungry, and worried. *Where could she be? She promised me! It was my time to say what I wanted and now she is nowhere to be found!*

The next morning, my mom still wasn't home. I sat there in the window and cried. I had no idea what was going on, or where she was. Could she have been one of the passengers in the ambulance that I saw the other night? I closed my eyes and just took myself to a place where I could control the outcome.

When I woke, my mom was standing there in the living room with boxes full of Mr. Goodbars™ and we sat there and drank milk and ate as many candy bars as we could until our bellies were full. I played her favorite song and we danced and sang. Then that part of the record came up where it started skipping, sounding like a loud, knocking sound. I asked her, could we skip that part, and she told me to hold on, it would fix itself.

"Don't worry, Lil Sheila, it will fix itself."

That's all I heard in my dream. That sound did not stop, it did not fix itself, it just kept getting louder and louder.

I woke up and could see that every time the knock came the door shook. I jumped up to run to my mom's room to wake her. I could not find her anywhere; I was so confused. We had just finished eating all of those Mr. Goodbars™ and the wrappers were everywhere, but now the floor was clean and the milk container and cups were gone.

I panicked! Someone was trying to break in and my mom was gone. I had to stay quiet and not let them know I was home alone. The knocking kept going and getting louder. I covered my ears and laid on my mom's bed with the cover over my head.

"Please, please go away," I whispered to myself. But the knocks kept getting louder and louder. I heard a voice yell out,

"Little Sheila, open the door. You are safe. We are here to help you."

I yelled back, "NO! My mom said not to open this door!"

They yelled back, "Your mom is with us at the police station, that's how we knew to come get you! Your mom got in some trouble and she is safe, but she needs us to keep you safe. She will be at the station for a little while and we are going to take you to a neighbor your mom knows in the next building who will watch you until she is able to come back home!"

We went back and forth for quite some time. Eventually, I gave in, opened the door and yes, it was the police. And yes, my mom was in trouble. (I later learned she got in trouble for shoplifting and trying to steal a camera.) I couldn't quite understand just what they were speaking of because my mom had promised me, she would be bringing back a Mr. Goodbar™.

I asked the police as they were entering our apartment,

"Did she give you my Mr. Goodbar™?"

They just stared at me blankly then walked past me. I asked again,

"Do you have my Mr. Goodbar™?"

Finally, one officer answered me, "I'm sorry, but we do not have any candy for you. Come on, let's go. It's time to leave and take you to your mom's friend's apartment now."

At that point, I was so upset I wanted to cry but could not. I still needed answers and no one would tell me.

Chapter 4
"In the closet"

They packed a small bag for me and they took me next door to a lady I didn't really know; I don't remember ever meeting her but she knew my mom. She had agreed to watch me until my mom was back home. When I arrived to her apartment, she told me to go sit down, no formal greetings or anything, just, "Sit down."

At the door, the police spoke to her for a minute and then left. I walked over to the place she directed me to go sit and saw a plate on the counter. I hadn't eaten in days and was so very hungry.

The lady had made some crackers with peanut butter on them and had them sitting on a plate on the counter. I snuck one, and then another, and, well, then another. I cannot recall exactly how many I ate, but it obviously was enough to see that several were gone. I sat there, still hungry, but it satisfied a bit of my hunger.

I was licking the last bit of peanut butter from my lips when all hell broke loose. The lady came over to the table, looked at the plate, then looked at me and started cursing.

"Who the hell told you that you could have some of these damned crackers? Did I tell you? Huh? Did I? Where's your manners? You don't just come into someone's home and start eating their food!"

I was shocked. I could not speak at all. I looked down at the floor, hoping if I didn't see her, she would just go away, but she didn't! She had turned into a monster right in front of my eyes. I didn't know I did something wrong. I was hungry, and she knew my mom was gone, so why did she get so angry? Before I knew it, she had called her son into the kitchen.

"Look what she done did! She ate up all of your crackers!"

She grabbed me by my long hair, whipped me around, slapped me, then her son proceeded to kick me. They opened a closet door and there were some boxes inside. The son stood on a box and unscrewed the light bulb from the socket in the ceiling of the closet. He pushed me into the closet and locked the door with a fancy, big key.

And there I sat, looking through the keyhole, watching them eat crackers and laugh. They were saying my name and telling me how good those crackers were.

"Lil Sheila....look at what we are eating! Do you want some? You can't have any!"

They kept antagonizing me; they would bring a cracker over to the keyhole and snatch it back.

I cried. I didn't say a word. I just cried. It was at that moment that I struggled to "take myself somewhere else" and pretend like everything was good. It wasn't. It was bad, and I had no idea that it was going to get worse. I did my best to hum a song to myself and envision that my mother would just show up and stop them from doing what they were doing to me.

She didn't and there I sat, in the dark, alone, hungry and scared.

At some point, the lady decided to bring me out of the closet. I was happy to see daylight and was hoping she had some food for me, but she didn't. She decided to bring me out and whip me for being bad earlier. I thought being in the closet was my punishment but I guess that wasn't enough.

She yelled at me, "You ate my crackers and you were not told to do so. You are being a bad little girl, Sheila!"

She used her hand, hitting me on my butt, legs, and back, then she grabbed a belt and continued to hit me and pull my hair. I screamed in complete pain and terror. I had no idea what I did that would result in this type of treatment. Her son grabbed my hair and hit me while his mother hit me with the belt. All the time I was screaming, they were using a red box of some type to record my screams.

I was begging them to stop, and telling them I was sorry and I wouldn't do it again. But they just laughed and continued to whip me and push me. I curled up in a ball crying, asking them to please stop. Eventually, they pushed me back into the closet, shut the door, and locked it.

Yes, I was back in the dark closet but it was better than being out there with them. I guess you could say, it was the lesser of two evils!

Again, I watched them through the keyhole as they played back my screams on that recorder and laughed at me and made faces towards the closet door.

I stood up against the door of the closet, my back was badly bruised and my butt hurt from all the hits. I couldn't move because I was in so much pain. I could not escape this torture at all.

No matter how hard I tried, I could only pay attention to what was happening. I thought about my mom and the police that had brought me there. I wished that someone would come and save me, but no one came. I wished they would have just left me alone at our apartment. I would have rather been alone and safe, than be where I was.

I don't know the amount of time that passed, but later they brought me out again. This time, they pulled my pants down and whipped my bare bottom, recorded my cries, and also took pictures.

I was so confused! Why did I deserve all of this for eating some crackers? This continued throughout the night and into the next day.

I thought I was going to die. I was in so much pain. I started drifting off between being tired, hungry, and scared. While standing, I rested my head against the door, almost in the spot near the keyhole. A breeze touched my nose, it started getting hot in the closet, and the cool breeze hypnotized me.

In dreamland... I could hear the ocean, or what I imagined it sounded like...sand on my bare feet as I stared off into the distance. The sun blinded me as I focused my eyes over the horizon to see that the water was full of people. They were all making their way out of the water in quite a hurry, and some of them had their mouths open as they pushed through the waves. As they got closer, some of them kept falling into the water and never coming back up. The closer they got to me, the louder they became, yelling and screaming. I could hear them now, loud and clear!

"Get up! Get. Up!"

Shocked that they were yelling at me, I flinched as they came running towards me and past me. They all had a look of fear in their eyes; whatever was chasing them was not that far behind. I could see the water starting to rise, a big wave was coming, and the more people screamed, the more of them were being swallowed up by the big wave.

I was paralyzed with fear and could not move. I could only watch as the people passed me, some with tears in their eyes and others bleeding from different areas of their bodies. As they passed me, I felt the saltwater that was dripping from them start to buildup on my shirt; their wet clothes drenched my shirt as they stood over me, panic-stricken.

They acted as if I wasn't even there. The wave of water was now even closer to me. Now it was blocking out the sun. It felt cold as the wind picked up. One by one, the wave swallowed all of the people who hadn't made it off the shoreline in time. I braced for impact.

I was stuck and could not move. I prayed that it would not get me. I laid down, holding my arms over my head. Then it happened. A loud crash! I felt the warmth from the sun again. Blinded, I heard it again,

"Get Up! Get Up! Wake your ass up!"

I was awakened by the lady pulling me by my hair and arm, dragging me out of the closet into the room. Everything was blurry. As I was trying to adjust my eyes, I could feel a sting on my back, and another one, and another one, until I blacked out, falling to the ground.

When I woke up again, I could feel something firm behind me, and my feet felt as if they were suspended and swinging. I was in a chair. I focused my eyes and could see the lady again, staring at me. She motioned to me with her hand, pointing at a plate.

"Earutagt! Earutagt! Eaaatt! Eat!"

As my ears were processing just what she was saying, my eyes adjusted to seeing her lips and her mouth squeezing hard as the words come through her lips. She demanded, "Eat!" as I looked over the plate with a half-cut sandwich, a piece of a cookie, and a few drops of juice in a cup.

I hesitated to reach for any of it, since the recent moments of my stay were absolute hell from eating the peanut butter crackers. She motioned to me again to take the sandwich and eat it. I slowly put the sandwich to my mouth, quickly devoured the rest, and sipped the drink.

She pushed me out of the chair and directed me to get back into the closet. I fell asleep and did not dream or think of anything. I was just exhausted.

I don't know how many days I was in that closet. If I had to guess, I would say about a week. I was let out to go to the bathroom and was given some water and something to snack on again, but then it was back to the same routine, back to the closet. In the beginning, I slept sitting up on the boxes, but eventually, I used a coat as a pillow and I slept on a box in the corner.

The whole time I was with that woman and her son, I remained in the dark closet, just staring out the keyhole, listening to them and watching them. It was so warm in there. The only air I could get was through the keyhole. I could see them, happy and laughing, eating and drinking, playing games, and there I sat, bruised, numb, and not even able to take myself to a happy place. I sat there quietly, rubbing my hands, crying, and watching them through the keyhole.

Why were they so mean to me? Why would my mom send me here? When is my mom coming back? Is she ever coming back? I can't wait to tell my mom how much I love her.

Finally, my mom showed up. Before she arrived, the woman and her son pulled me from the closet, took a rag and wiped my face, brushed my hair and told me they would kill me if I said a word to anyone.

Trust me, I was only five. They had beaten and tortured me enough that I was afraid of them, and I didn't doubt what they said! I thought Bill was mean to my mom, but this lady had Bill beat. She was a whole new level of "monster."

As my mom and I were walking away, the lady was so nice. She smiled at me and told me to be a good little girl, and she told my mom if she ever needed her again to watch me, just let her know.

I held my mom's hand tightly as we walked back to our apartment. I could have almost died with what I was feeling inside. I wanted so badly to tell my mom what had happened to me, but she ruled the conversation.

"Now, Little Sheila, listen, I need you to be a big girl and understand somethings that I have to tell you, okay? Now, Mommy has got herself into a little bit of trouble. I don't know what's gonna happen. I have to go to court soon, because I was caught doing something bad. This means that I have to send you away to stay with either some friends or..."

She stopped as she was searching for the words and tapping on her knee. Whatever it was, it was something that she was having a hard time dealing with. She started off again,

"Mommy is gonna have to find you somewhere to live, because you won't be able to stay with me. Mommy is going away for a while."

After she finished with that, she stopped, wiped a tear from her eye, and postured up very quickly. She made a phone call, then another one, and then the last one. She sank back in the chair. She stared up at the ceiling for a while.

"Sheila, I may be going to jail..."

She stared at me and started crying, then again, jumped up with excitement as she thought of who I could stay with. She started making calls again and sank back into her chair. She stared at the phone and took a deep breath and made another call. She had a long conversation with the person on the phone.

I could hear her say, "Sheila needs a place to go for a while." And there were a lot of "Huh," "Hush," "You have to believe me!" and "Fine!"

The conversation ended and my mother told me I was going to go live with my grandparents in Dowagiac, MI. I later learned that my grandparents had never seen me and they weren't really thrilled with the idea of my coming there, but my mother assured them it would only be for a short time.

Later that night, after eating dinner, my mom told me to get ready to take a bath. Hearing those words, I was frightened, *Ohh no, she will see the marks on my back and that lady and her son will kill me!*

"Little Sheila! Come on, come take a bath!"

I hid near my couch; I didn't want my mom to find out about all the marks I had on me from staying with her friend.

"Little Sheila? Where are you?"

My mom called out to me as she walked from the bathroom to my hiding place.

"What are you doing?"

She looked down at me with her baby blue eyes, admiring me, and then the look in her eyes turned to concern.

"What's wrong Little Sheila? Tell me what's wrong!"

I responded, "Nothing."

As she took my clothes off to give me a bath and wash my hair, she noticed the marks on my back. She asked me what happened and I lied. I told her I got hurt playing Double-Dutch jump rope.

I guess she knew better, so she asked me again and again,

"Sheila, what happened? This is worse than jump rope marks."

I told her, "I don't want to die. I can't tell you!"

She replied, "Little Sheila, you are not going to die. Why would you say such a thing?"

I dropped my head down and stared at the bathwater. I remained silent. She gently lifted up my chin to look into her eyes and she asked again,

"Sheila, please tell me what happened."

In the end, I did tell her, and I don't know what happened, but she stormed out that door, told me to lock it, and said to not let anyone in but her.

She came back a short time later. She was mad and crying and she kept saying,

"I have to get you out of here. I'm so sorry, Little Sheila, I'm so, so sorry."

And she hugged me for a long time. I could hear the fear and anger in her voice as she held me. She was shaking, which made me upset and I cried in her arms. This reminded me of the times that she was beaten and bruised by Bill, but this time was different. There was no music playing. She did not lip-sync to any rhythm and blues tunes. There was no dancing around with a wooden hairbrush handle mic. There was nothing but tears.

I think I cried myself to sleep because when I woke, I was still in her arms. She just looked at me, stroking my forehead and moving my hair out of my face. She told me that all of my stuff was ready and packed and that I would be going on a long trip to see my grandparents. She gave me a set of new rules: Not to talk to any strangers and to pay close attention to my surroundings.

I thought to myself, *I could do it just like I did it around the apartment.*

She spent time telling me how my new home would be different from our apartment, and that she would come to get me later after she had straightened out her issues. She promised me she would be back to get me.

Chapter 5
"Moving Day"

The next morning, I woke up, laying in my mom's bed. I can still remember how soft the bed and pillows were. I buried my head into the pillow covered with a lilac flower design. It felt cool around my head and ears. I took a deep breath and could smell the perfume my mother had worn a couple of days back lingering in the sheet and pillowcase.

With another deep breath and long stretch, I found myself all alone in the bed. As I wrestled with the piles of sheets on the bed, another scent hit my nose. It made my stomach and taste buds do a dance.

The house was filled with all types of aromas, some I was familiar with, and others I had never smelled. Finally, I made it out of bed and started walking down the hallway, being led by such succulent scents that I could taste what was cooking.

"Little Sheila, good morning. I made you some breakfast."

I didn't know if this was a dream or reality because, most times, I was the one in charge and had to make breakfast for myself and Charlotte; our breakfast consisted of milk and cereal, nothing too fancy.

She had cooked me breakfast! Bacon, eggs, toast with cheese, butter, and jelly. *This has to be the best day of my life,* I was thinking while settling myself at the table, getting my mouth ready for this feast. I grabbed my plate and pulled it close to me while taking in a spoonful of eggs. They tasted so good and buttery, the cheese so gooey, all of this food hit the spot.

My mom stood near the window sipping on coffee and looking back at me as I ate. She would give me a smile in between asking me,

"Little Sheila, is it good?"

I just nodded my head each time with my mouth full. I was so hungry I could've eaten a horse, and maybe a pig or two, just no cockroaches! I was quickly emptying the plate in front of me when my mother interrupted me, saying,

"Little Sheila, finish, I have to get you to the bus stop in time."

She paced around nervously as she lit a cigarette and looked out the window.

Just looking at her, I could feel her excitement, fear, and uncertainty all at once. She stared back at me while smoking her cigarette.

I wanted so badly to tell her, "Don't worry Mom, it will be okay," but I couldn't, because I was only five years old. What did I know about the next second, minute, hour, or day in life? I was living one day at a time.

I was finally finished and she came over, wiped my face, and looked at me again.

"My beautiful baby...." she just stopped talking and started crying.

I wondered just what was going on in her head, because one moment she was happy, the next moment she was sad. It was for sure an emotional rollercoaster for her. I was just playing in my head what she was telling me.

"It will be just for a little while, until everything blows over, and then I will come back to get you," she said with a quiver in her voice.

It was time to go. She had packed a small suitcase with some undershirts, underwear, one or two outfits, a doll, a couple of other small items, and my blue coat trimmed in white. I remember my outfit as if it were yesterday: It was a horizontal-striped shirt with a pair of light blue pants that had a crease going up the middle of each leg.

With a safety pin on the front of my shirt, she attached an envelope with this address on it: 342 Pokagon St. Dowagiac, MI. She included about four pictures and a note inside. We walked to the bus station and this was where she told me I was going away, alone. She said she would not be going with me.

Again, she said she was sorry but she was in big trouble. She would be going to jail and I needed to be a big girl and do this trip alone.

"Don't worry, Little Sheila you will be staying with your grandparents," she said. "They know you are coming and this nice bus driver (a colored man) will make sure you get there safely."

She slipped the little blue coat trimmed in white in my arms, then she handed me my suitcase and sent me on my way, up the bus steps. The nice bus driver introduced himself, shook my hand, and told me what a pleasure it was to meet me. He seated me right behind his seat and he took my suitcase and my coat and put them up on a shelf above my head. He told my mom he would make sure I got to Dowagiac safely.

She hugged him and thanked him and waved goodbye to me and stepped back off the bus. She was crying the whole time. She looked so sad.

The strange thing? I didn't cry. I was excited and happy. Maybe I felt, *anything would be better than this,* so I was just looking forward to the journey. I don't know, but I wasn't that little girl who cried and begged my mom to stay with me.

All I'd ever known was to be independent: "Little Sheila do this, Little Sheila do that, make sure you lock the door, cook and clean..."

I had gained some form of independence. I trusted what my mother told me and I was ready for this journey. As the bus started pulling away, I could see my mom waving and crying, until about halfway down the street I could not see her anymore. I just saw cars and buildings passing by.

This was my very first time being on a big bus, sitting by the window, looking out as we passed the buildings. *This is going to be fun.*

The bus driver introduced himself,

"Hi, Little Sheila, I am Stan. Nice to meet you."

I smiled and replied, "Hello, Mr. Stan, I am Little Sheila. Nice to meet you!"

"You seem like a happy little girl," the bus driver said. "We are going to have a fun ride to your grandparents' house, so sit back and enjoy the ride. We will be making one stop along the way."

I nodded my head and put up two fingers, just like the peace sign, saying,

"Aye-aye, Captain!"

He laughed and turned around.

For some reason, I had no fear! I mean, I was sad to leave my mom standing there at the bus station, but I was excited, and as strange as it may seem, I felt safe.

Am I really safe? I mean, here I am, a little girl, on this bus with a bunch of strangers, and some man driving the bus, and he is in charge of my safe delivery to Dowagiac, MI, which is approximately a two-hour drive.

We were driving along and I was in awe with all the buildings, all the cars, and all the people. I couldn't sit up tall enough in my seat! I was on the edge of it and looking over the bus driver's shoulder. I couldn't stop smiling.

I imagined meeting my grandparents and them meeting me with open arms, they being just as excited seeing me as I am seeing them. While looking out the window and watching all of the buildings go by, I started daydreaming.

My mom had said they lived in a house. I never lived in a house, only an apartment, so I wondered what that house would look like.

A house...with lots of space, enough space for everyone, no sleeping on couches or floors, big, nice, comfortable beds with nice, cool sheets. A great kitchen with pantries full of food, a fully-working stove with all its buttons and handles intact, a big refrigerator full of food, all types

40

of meats and cold drinks, and an unlimited amount of Mr. Goodbars™! Especially no Killer Cockroaches!

I came to... looking around to see if we had made it to my grandparents' house.

I don't know how much time passed, but we eventually stopped at a gas station for a break to go to the bathroom and get a pop. The bus driver told me to stay put in my seat and asked me if I wanted a Coke®. I told him I did.

I was feeling a little cold. He walked off the bus, but I was confused, besides being a little cold. My coat was up above me on that shelf with my suitcase. I wondered, *why is he leaving the bus to get my coat?* (I guess even in my younger years I was hard of hearing. He said "Coke®," but I heard "coat.")

Anyway, he returned with the biggest Coke® I had ever seen. I sat back in my seat and I grabbed that big cup of Coke® and I couldn't stop thinking how fun this was.

I drank it all; I drank more than I should have. I drank it fast, and after the last sip, I threw up all over the front of my shirt and on the back of the driver's seat.

It was at this point that I panicked and crawled under the seat. I knew I was going to be in trouble.

Mr. Stan pulled the bus over, grabbed some rags, and talked me out from under the seat.

"Little Sheila," he said, "come out from under there so I can help you clean up. Yes, it's ok, we all make boo-boos every now and then."

He chuckled as he extended his hand to me. He cleaned me off and cleaned up the seat and the floor, and a couple of other people came up front to help him. I was getting myself "mentally ready" to be whipped or yelled at, but he never did. He was still nice to me. I found myself happy again, and even though I smelled of puke, I was still smiling.

Back on the road again I could see fewer buildings by now, just wide-open spaces and plenty of trees. I had never seen so many trees and stretches of land as far as the eye could see.

"We will be in Dowagiac in another five minutes," said a voice over the loudspeaker at the same time Mr. Stan was speaking.

I looked at the road and surrounding area; it looked nothing like I had pictured it in my daydream and I wondered where all the people were.

We pulled into a gas station and there stood a lady wearing bright red lipstick and leaning against a taxi. The first thing I noticed about her was her bright lips!

The bus driver told me to stay seated, let the other people off, and then he would get my suitcase and coat. He did say, "coat," this time and not "Coke®."

It was finally my turn to get off. He held my hand and walked me off the bus, then he introduced himself to the lady with the bright red lips. She looked at me and said,

"Hi, Little Sheila."

And I responded with "Hi" and asked if she was gonna be my mom. She replied,

"Yes, I am your grandma and I will be taking care of you for a while."

The bus driver handed over my things and told her about the puke incident. They laughed, we said our goodbyes, then into the taxi we went.

Chapter 6
"My Grandparents"

The drive was short. I later understood that we lived only about a mile out of downtown, so I spent most of the time in the cab starring at my grandma's lips.

She would look out the window and then back at me and give me a smirk, then back to the window. I studied her face, wondering if I had ever seen her before in my life. *Who am I fooling, I'm only five!* She didn't look like my mother; this woman had a smaller nose and tiny lips that stretched across her face, meeting high cheekbones at each corner. I paid very close attention to her lips as I stared at them intently. I asked her,

"Do they hurt?"

She looked down at me, puzzled, then looked around the taxi, out the window, and then back at me, confused. She looked down at her watch and shook her arm and responded.

"No, Baby Sheila, they do not hurt at all," she said, peering down at me with a smirk.

I pointed at her ruby red lips as they poked out, "No... those! They look like they hurt!"

She was visibly offended; her smirk turned into a frown as she took a stern look at me. She reached out to me and squeezed my arm hard, with enough force that it almost made me cry. She released it and didn't say a word. The look on her face showed me she did not approve of my question.

Turning back to look out of the window, she raised her hand and pointed in the direction of the road. I concentrated on the drive, and it wasn't long before we were pulling into a long driveway and up to a big house.

WOW... this looks so different than Chicago.

I got out, taking it all in. The house was red with white window frames, with a detached garage barn, and trees everywhere. There was one beautiful tree that I just loved and I asked my grandma,

"What's that tree over there?"

She replied, "That's called a weeping willow tree, Sheila."

That would become my favorite spot in the yard, sitting under that tree, and the yard was so big. The driveway was part grass and gravel and very long.

I took in a deep breath. It was all new to me. Even the air smelled different. Turning around, I watched the taxi backing down the gravel drive, leaving behind a big cloud of dust as it kicked up rocks until it got to the street.

I had never seen such a big house. There were other houses around, but not real close like the apartments in Chicago. I could see the neighbors' houses, separated by a sea of tall grass.

I was so excited! *I wish my mom could see this*, I thought to myself. I wondered what my Double-Dutch friends would think about a place like this. We could Double-Dutch without worrying about the next car pulling in or out of the parking lot, or even anyone bothering us.

I gazed off, thinking about them all arriving in the same taxi that dropped us off. We played and had so much fun, then they all disappeared.

I could imagine my mom with a smile on her face, relaxed and happy.

"Little Sheila!" she yelled out as she made her way up the stairs to give me a hug.

"Mommy! I missed you! Now we can live in this big house and not have to worry about anything!"

I reached out to hug her and felt nothing, I looked up and she was no longer there. I could hear a voice yelling at me from inside the house.

"Baby Sheila! Come here, let me take a look at you."

It was a man's voice and it startled me at first. I didn't expect to hear it, but it was my grandfather. My grandmother came back out the door and motioned for me to come in.

I slowly walked in the door and immediately smelled something so strong it almost knocked me off my feet. My eyes started to itch and my throat starting hurting. While I tried to clear the smell out of my nose I started sneezing. My grandmother hurried into the kitchen, where I could see some smoke coming from the stove.

"Ohh nooo," my grandfather screamed from his chair "You forgot to turn off the oven, Ines!"

"Yes, I forgot, I didn't think the bus was going to take that long to get here."

My grandmother pulled a pie out of the oven and put it in the sink, then she ran water over it. The house was filled with smoke, and she started opening the windows to let it all out.

She and my grandfather came out to the front porch and told me to take a seat outside as she cleared the house of the smoke.

"What a way to meet your grandparents," my grandfather said to me, smiling as we sat on the porch.

It took a while for the smoke to clear out of the house, so during that time we got to know each other. I had millions of questions, some they answered and some when they changed the subject.

I asked, "Why are you upset with my mom?"

They didn't respond but changed the subject.

"Ohh, Baby Sheila, we are not upset with your mom, we are helping her out. We love you."

"Baby Sheila, I heard you are a good dancer and you love jumping rope," my grandmother interrupted.

"Yes! My friends taught me how to jump rope called Double-Dutch and they showed me this new dance."

I showed them a dance I had just learned called the "popcorn dance." They laughed and I got even sillier. They really enjoyed watching me dance and act silly. My grandfather told me he had a talent also.

"Can you go get me my box, Ines?"

He directed my grandmother to go get a box from inside by the fireplace. By then the smoke had cleared from the house.

She came back with a box and it was brown, white and red. He pulled out two things and started to use them against his leg and shoulder. He was good at it. I asked him,

"What do you call those things?"
He told me they were called "bones" and he explained to me how they worked.

"Bones!" I yelled. I had heard the guys down at the park talk about that, and even sometimes fight when they were playing the game. I explained to my grandparents about what the guys would do back in my old neighborhood in Chicago. The looks on their faces told me they had no idea what I was talking about.

My grandfather started to show me all the different ways to play the bones.

"Come here, Baby Sheila."

Before he could finish, I corrected him,

"No, I'm Little Sheila!"

My grandfather turned red with embarrassment and said, "Ohh, okay, sorry Little Sheila!"

He sat back in his chair and started to chuckle to himself.

"Look at my hands and how I hold the bones. This will help me make great sounds and allow me to shake my hands and then comes the sounds."

He held on to two bones and separated them in his hands, between his fingers, and them not touching. He began to play and he played them for a long time. He even sang a song while he played. He started talking about all the ways to play the bones.

"Singles, doubles, fours and threes, and reels, one, two, three, four, let's mix it up!"

He was so excited teaching me how to play bones. He knew what he was doing and I just watched in amazement. I asked him where he got them and he told me some were from the store and others were leftovers from ribs.

"Ribs? Ohh nooo!"

"Little Sheila, don't be scared! They make them in all types of material so you can get them in metal, wood, stone, or from a dead animal. No animals were harmed at all, from my understanding."

As he raised his hands and showed me a set, he said, "I found these in a field while I was a kid walking back from school. I cleaned them up and started practicing with them. I worked with what I had."

"Later, when I was grown, I was able to buy some new bones from the store. These," he said, raising his hands and showing them off to me.

I felt like the center of attention; my grandparents spoke to me for so long that day, and it seemed like they wanted to get to know everything about me. And I wanted to know just as much about them. We excitedly shared other stories with each other, and things that we knew how to do. Every time I brought up my mom's name, they would change the subject and just seem to want to focus on me and what I was like.

It had been a long first day and I became sleepy. My grandmother showed me where I was going to sleep. I followed her to the room. It was a big room, to the left of the bathroom. It had a grand bed in the middle of it and it had more covers on it than my mother's bed. My grandmother had to help me get into the bed.

I was so used to sleeping on the couch, so this felt just like heaven! This was a big bed and she pinned the sheets down on each side with big safety pins so I was kind of locked in. She didn't want me to fall out of the bed.

I remember the sounds and the moon shining in the window. The surroundings were so different. So quiet. No people yelling. No music. No sirens. I was used to always hearing sirens going to the hospital across the street, sirens from the police cars and firetrucks. Here, it was quiet and calm.

For the first time in a long time, I woke up dry... I didn't pee the bed. I woke up the next morning and my grandmother came to unwrap me. I was happy to see her and even happier when my bed was not wet.

My grandmother let me help with making breakfast and do work around the yard. Before I knew it, the weekend was over and my grandma had to go to work.

My grandma worked at a bait factory and we didn't have a car. We would walk a mile to town to get groceries, then we'd walk that mile back, both of us carrying bags. We'd stop along the way for breaks. My grandfather didn't go with us; he was ill and didn't work. It was always just me and Grandma.

We had to be careful. My grandfather told me we would be walking through a bad area, where there would be a lot of "colored people" outside.

"Don't talk to them," he told me. "Don't make eye contact. Just keep walking."

I understood not to talk to strangers; my mother taught me that very well in our apartment. But I didn't see it being a problem to say hello if I saw a little girl or boy my age. But my grandfather did not approve and I did not want to make him mad.

This was definitely a different lifestyle. I lived with my grandparents for a few years.

I didn't have many friends in this area; most of them were colored and I was not allowed to play with them. I explained that I played Double-Dutch jump rope with the girls in Chicago and they were very nice.

My grandpa said, "If I see you talking to them, you will be grounded, and you will go pick a switch off of the tree, and you will get three whacks with a switch. You can talk to the white neighbor girl next door, Rosalynn, but you can't play at their house."

What a culture shock! I was comfortable back in Chicago playing with my "colored" friends, *but now, why is it a crime,* I kept thinking to myself.

I could only imagine what my mom went through when she was younger and living with her parents. The area that they stayed in was a majority colored, and they forbade me to speak to any of them. I had good experiences with them when I lived in Chicago but here it was another story.

My grandparents had disowned my mom. They were aware of her ways of being a prostitute, and free and easy, dealing with the colored folks, and it was "the 60's for God's sake." They really didn't talk to her that much, so to get them to take me in was quite a chore.

I remember hearing her on the phone with them. She had numerous conversations trying to persuade them to take me. They finally caved and agreed to take me, but I guess it was against their better judgment.

They really didn't know what they were going to get, my mom staying with a colored man and all. My grandparents argued with my mother, stating,

"You want us to take her when I know who she looks like? She's mixed, she's not white!"

So, when I showed up and I was a pale, white girl with long, blonde hair and hazel eyes, I'm sure they were relieved. They really didn't want me, but I needed somewhere to go. Even though they didn't meet me until I was five years old, I felt like we had known each other all those five years of my life.

Things were so different, but I was very happy that my grandparents didn't abuse me. They were older and had no idea how to deal with a five-year-old, soon a six-year-old.

As I got older, my grandma would go to Woolworth's™ and buy me toys made for kids who were five, but I was now 10! She did finally get me the *Farmer's See N Say,* and she always got me a Mr. Goodbar™ when we went to town.

She was different but, I found her funny. Her actions and facial expressions made me giggle.

She tried, to raise me right, but she would overdo it. If I wore shorts in the summer, they were down to my kneecaps, with socks to my knees, and long-sleeved shirts. I couldn't sit on the concrete steps because I could get a "cold in my bowels." Wisdom from old folks.

One thing that still sticks with me is the first time I really made her angry. There was a big dirt pile outside, and my grandma had bought me a very pretty Sarah Coventry ring with flowers on it. I didn't have it long, because I was digging in the dirt pile and I lost it. I remember her being very upset with me; she had spent a lot of money on that ring and I didn't take care of it.

That was when I finally heard her yell at me. You see, my grandmother was the mild-mannered one; my grandfather was the firecracker.

My grandfather was so different than my grandma. He didn't like visitors and when people would stop by unannounced, he would go into his room, pretend like he was sleeping, and he would tell me to tell them that he was laying down resting.

My grandfather had high blood pressure, CHF (congestive heart failure), and trouble hearing. I think he was embarrassed by this; he just chose to not "engage" rather than struggle to follow along in conversation. His personality was so different than my grandmother's. I've always wondered how they ended up together, but they say opposites attract.

Chapter 7
"A lonely existence"

Talk about culture shock, yes, I experienced a cultural and life-changing shock, if that even exists. Living with my grandparents was night and day different from where I'd come from. All of the things that I did in Chicago I did not do in Dowagiac, MI. There was a lot of adjusting to the new life that I was living.

I spent a lot of time by myself. Because my grandparents were older, they could not spend a lot of time with me. My grandmother was still working and my grandfather stayed around the house; he would watch Lawrence Welk, Western shows, and I Love Lucy, listen to Dixieland music, or play his bones. Eventually, he let me play the Stroh's beer bottles with an ink pen while he played the bones. I'm pretty sure nobody would hire us!

He loved to do yard work. It would take him hours to push mow the yard, over the hill and down to the creek. I would sit outside under the weeping willow tree, listen to the radio, and watch the birds entering the martin birdhouses that he had built. He especially loved his Four O'clock flowers in all the different colors; they grew so tall and full. He would make me collect the seeds and put them in a jar to plant later.

I spent a lot of time outside, playing make-believe. My usual way of coping with trauma in my life had taken a front seat. I was in an uncomfortable place now. I could not talk to anyone and my longing for my mother kept me in a strange place. My grandparents did not help the situation at all, with a lot of their old-fashioned rules and fears.

I began to go inside myself; I guess it was the best way I knew to deal with things, make sense of things, and the only true way to survive.

My grandparents had a library in a room upstairs but I was not allowed to go upstairs. The walls had built-in shelves and drawers that were full of books. I would always try to sneak upstairs and look through the books on the shelves and in the drawers.

One day I opened the bottom drawer and discovered those books were for my grandpa. They had naked women in them. I quickly closed that drawer and never said a word to anyone. I never opened the bottom drawer again!

Sometimes, my grandmother worked long hours at the factory, and on this day, she was working another long shift. I said to myself, *now is the time!* I opened the door and I walked upstairs when I knew that my grandpa was outside and busy building something in the barn.

I snuck into the room! It not only had lots of shelves with books, but also a record player and an entertainment center with records.

I started my search down the bookshelf and then one book stood out and caught my attention. It had a bird and a mouse on the cover; the mouse sat on the bird's wing as it flew. I was intrigued by this book. It looked new and I opened the pages to look through it. The pages were easy to open and I noticed some notes written inside the first couple of pages.

"Record and read to Little Sheila"

It was in my grandmother's signature, I noticed; I'd seen her write on pieces of paper when we would walk to the store and this was just like that handwriting.

I looked around and found a large recorder behind me on the shelf near the other wall. I knew it was a recorder; it was similar to the one that my mom's friend had when they used it to record me crying while they laughed. But this recorder was black, not red like the one she had in that apartment.

On a table, I found a cassette that was identical to the book I held in my hand. I put it in the player and pushed buttons to start the cassette. Immediately, I jumped back; the voice coming out of the player was my grandmother's.

"*Mrs. Frisby and the Rats of NIMH*...Chapter One."

She began to read the book and I listened as I stared at the cover of the book and wondered what a bird and a mouse had to do with each other.

I snuck back upstairs every day that my grandmother worked late and listened to her read the book. I was excited to see my name in the book and on the recording. She never had time to read to me, and this was quite a surprise.

I had found an escape for the time being. I was always alone and had to make up stories on my own. I fell in love with this book, hearing that the condition of the characters almost mirrored my life. I could relate to the feelings of despair and hopelessness that the main character was dealing with.

She needed to find a way to get her children to safety and is promised that there is a chance the Rats can help her.

I felt hopeless at one point while I listened. I realized that my mother had not contacted me and I was waiting on her to come back and pick me up.

Months passed. One day, my mother finally called, and my grandparents told me that she was coming to visit. She came and stayed with us for a couple of days. I thought that I would be leaving with her when it was time for her to leave. She convinced me that she would be back. She said she would be gone for a little while and would come back soon.

As the weeks became months and the months became years, my hope started to deplete. My vision of us being a happy family, me being with my mother, started to become a mission impossible.

I was never able to finish the rest of the book; where I left off was in uncertainty. The main character was still trying to get help and it seemed like no one would help her in time.

In my real life, I waited also, but help never came. I was again alone. Even though I lived with my grandparents, it still felt like I was back in the apartment, looking out for myself. The older I became, the more it seemed evident that I was not anyone's main priority.

I was made to feel like I was in a room full of people and still was alone. No one really cared about me, or there was something I wanted but couldn't have, my mother. Try explaining to a child why her mother didn't want her. Had I been so bad? Am I that ugly?

No matter what I read or the things I did to keep myself occupied, I still had a void in my life. I spent the majority of my days outside during those years, learning to twirl a baton, kicking a ball in the air and catching it, drawing the layout of houses in the dirt, and then jumping from one square to another square, pretending I was going from the kitchen to the living room. Playing alone in my imaginary world became my new normal. One thing was for sure, we didn't talk about my mother and it was apparent, she wasn't coming back.

Chapter 8
"School Days"

My grandparents did not help me with my homework. I was on my own and elementary school was hard. I was awkward. My grandma would dress me in dresses down to my knees and socks up to my knees, just like those shorts and socks in the summer. On a good note, I had the tannest kneecaps in town!

Anyway, school truly sucked. I didn't fit in. On the school bus, I was picked on a lot because there were mostly colored kids on the bus and my grandpa had told me I wasn't supposed to talk to them. That made it worse.
They'd say:

"What's wrong?"

"Cat got your tongue?"

"Are you scared?"

"Oh, she doesn't know how to talk, she was bird poop on a rock and hatched."

"She's retarded."

"You are so ugly your own parents don't want you!"

They would pull my hair and call me names. One girl who lived down the street would always spit in my hair and threaten to cut it off. It seemed like the bus ride took forever. Once I made it to school, it wasn't as bad.

Believe me, I had a few choice words for them, but in the beginning, it was eating me up. I needed to explain but

I held my tongue, because my grandparents scared me into thinking that the coloreds weren't people at all, they were more like the Boogie Man or a wild and deranged animal.

Ohh, how I wanted to explain! My feelings were hurt and I didn't want my grandparents to be right. I figured it was rude if someone spoke to you and you didn't say a word back, so I tried to use that as an excuse.

But why did I listen to them? Why was I so rude? I have brought all of this on myself and I needed to save myself and do it fast!

The next morning, while walking to the bus stop, I was good and ready! I had rehearsed my lines overnight. It was "go time" and I was ready!

"Excuse me...I know I haven't spoken to you all yet. I apologize, it wasn't me... let me explain. You ever hear of "mutism?" Yes, it's very rare (well it's quite common) but forget all of that! I suffered from it just last week! I was talking a lot and my gramps was like, 'Girl, don't you ever shut up?' He said it so loud and angry, I had to ask myself, 'Do you ever shut up?' and I was like, 'No.' So it had me thinking that if it made my gramps that mad, I didn't want to get anyone else that angry again, so I decided not to. Sooo... that's why I didn't say anything to you! See! Problem solved, and we can now be friends!"

The statement must've put everyone in shock, because when I looked up, I saw faces just staring, not just a blank stare, but stares with anticipation. They were hanging on to my every word, waiting to hear all of my wonderful stories... and then it happened.

My friend, whom I talked to every now and then on the bus, stood in front of me and waved her hand across my face,

"Hey, are you ok? Anyone home in there? The bus is here let's go!"

Apparently, no one heard a word that I said; I could just as well have been talking to myself!

I swear that was my experience; every time I tried to say something prolific, nothing ever came out. The worst parts of elementary school were the "functions," i.e., Parent's Day, the Daddy-Daughter Dance, Grandparent's Day, the breakfast and lunch days.

Since I didn't have a mom or dad, and my grandparents wouldn't be caught dead speaking with, let alone eating with, some "coloreds," I was all by myself. I remember there were "trade days with your parents" when you'd go to work with them. My teacher would sub in as my parent and we would have great conversations as we reminisced about what we were going to do on the coming weekend once we got home from school. Parents would come in to have lunch with their kids and I had nobody. Most of the time, the teacher would come to sit with me.

The days we would have Show-N-Tell, I would sneak my grandpa's bones out of his case and take them to school.

"Today's Show-N-Tell class, we have Lil Sheila!"

Remember, no one ever really heard me speak, so it was a grand surprise to them that I could speak at all, let alone play bones and sing.

It was my time and I was going to show them my true talent! I took my position in front of the class and gathered myself and the bones out of my bag.

I started out with a few taps of bones between my fingers and began to sing,

"Dem bones, dem bones, dem bones...dudutudududutuuuu! The foot bones connected to the leg bone; the leg bone is connected to the knee bone; the knee bone is connected to the thigh bone, doing the bones dannnccceee!"

And the class went wild! It was pure pandemonium, I tell you! Each kid jumped up and sang along with me as the teacher struggled to keep the classroom quiet and gets 29 rowdy 8-year olds back to their seats.

I returned to my seat with a huge smile on my face as the children around me kept repeating the catchy tune until they stopped singing and returned back to their seats. It was fabulous, like the Hokey Pokey meets the bones; I enjoyed every minute until it stopped. Then I heard a voice.

"Lil Sheila! Do you have anything to share with us today?"

I didn't, the bones never left the house and I never left my seat. I just shook my head and she continued on to the next student.

That's how my elementary school years went. I got used to not sharing those times with a parent figure and I think I started to resent my grandparents.

I always wanted to play with one of my childhood friends I met; she would only talk on the bus. Knowing how my grandparents felt about me talking, or even playing with "colored children," I became depressed. We would make plans about what we would do when we got home, but we never were able to do so.

I would imagine her being at my house playing with me. Other than the little girl Rosalynn, who lived next door, I had nobody to play with. My grandparents didn't really care for her family, so playtime was limited. I could only see her once in a blue moon.

Once I got into junior high school, my aunt and uncle stepped up to take on the task of raising me. I wanted to get active in things and my grandparents had no way to get me to and from activities.

I did become active in school. I played softball in the city league, I was a pompom girl, but I also was learning life without my mom. My aunt and uncle talked with my grandparents and the transition took place. Sounds like a great idea doesn't it? Except my aunt was only nine years older than me. She had no kids. Needless to say, there was a lot of turmoil there.

I was now free from staying to myself and I wanted to spread my wings and seek out new friends.

I was always in trouble. I was always told to be home when the streetlights came on, you know, "If you're not home when the street lights come on, you're gonna be in trouble." I didn't take the threat; it went in one ear and out the other.

Yeah, I don't know what they thought would work. They didn't know how to talk to me and I didn't make it easy. I didn't listen and, quite frankly, I knew it all!

I continued to get in trouble and of course, we had our fair share of fights and confrontations. It took me many years to realize my aunt and uncle were trying, but they struggled with how to handle someone like me.

Yeah, what do you think would happen when you're alone so much of your life when you're younger? Then you've got these people trying to give you rules. So, there will be some pushback. My aunt and uncle were busy. She cut hair and he worked at a local factory. They truly tried to guide me, but I was hellbent on doing it my way.

When I moved in with them, I felt free and happy because we had a car, they were not as old as my grandparents, and this was going to be fun. It was fun sometimes but not always. They had rules and well... I rebelled. I became very argumentative.

Once I got into junior high, things kind of changed; those kids thought I was lucky. I didn't have parents to yell at me and ground me. The bonus was that now I was no longer a mute, I spoke, and by then I could not shut up!

One of my childhood classmates from 3rd grade finally got up enough courage to speak to me and apologize.

"Hey, Lil Sheila, how are you doing? I know we have not been the best of friends when we were in elementary school, and I know most people thought that you were either a mute, or thought you were better than us since you are white. But I just wanted to say I felt bad about what those kids did to you that one year. I know you wanted to fight them, they picked on me also. I hated them."

We were partnered up in science class to do a project together, so it forced her to speak to me. I actually liked it! It gave me a chance to really let her know what was on my mind and prove to her that I was not a mute, dumb, or a poor little white girl playing the victim.

"Hey, by the way, don't call me 'Lil Sheila.' That is not my name. It's just Sheila ok! And for starters, yes, I can talk, mostly to myself, but I can talk. I'm originally from Chicago and my mom brought me here to live with my grandmother and grandfather until she gets herself together."

She told me about herself and we shared plenty of stories about one another. And it was crazy, because, for the most part, our stories were the same. I started to speak with her more, and she introduced me to some classmates that I wouldn't have dared speak to in elementary school. There were even some who had done some God-awful things to me on the bus. I could tell that they were a bit nervous at first, but we became associates, not as much as friends, but we were cool.

I had finally arrived! I had a good mixture of friends from all races, even though the outside world was going to hell in a handbasket when it came to race relations. I figured if you were cool with me, I was cool with you. I was on a quest to find myself, or discover my new self and the world around me, and nothing or no one was gonna get in my way.

Hanging out with my friends, I was being well-cultured in this thing called rock-n-roll; oh, what a glorious sound. Back then, you had all types of bands and solo acts who seemed like they were in my head and understood just what I was feeling at any given moment in my life!

As you would say, I came a little late to the party; most of my friends knew all of the new music coming out and the latest dances. Being around old people and listening to old folk songs and very old music made me, a budding teenager, old before my time!

One day during lunch, a friend of mine had brought a record to school and we snuck into the media center to play it. We got in and were able to unlock the record player. Once she put that record on, it changed my life!

The song started playing, the flicker of the piano keys sent vibrations through my soul, it was the beautiful keystrokes for me...der-na...dernaderna derna der-neer, ding der near ding near ding derna ding ding.... *"Lady! When you're with me I'm smiling, Give me. Aallalalalalalalayaa your Loooooveee!"* I must've died and gone straight to heaven! I could see it!

Angels with tiny little wings on their backs, and with golden harps, just playing and floating along. I asked myself, *how in the world are they able to hold those ginormous harps and stay afloat with those tiny wings? They were angels, for Pete's sake! But never mind, they just can, ok?*

Streams of chocolate-covered loveliness, chased by mounds of butter-covered peanuts... Note to self: that didn't come out the way I was thinking it, but you get the gist. It was pure sweetness.

That moment, my stomach started growling. We had skipped lunch to sneak off and listen to this record. Lucky for me, all my chocolate dreams came true, because I had a half-melted Mr. Goodbar™ in my coat pocket.

We ran out of the room once we heard some noise coming down the hallway. My friend never was able to go back and retrieve her record. Years later, I was able to get up enough money to find the record and send it to her for her 16th birthday. What a wonderful surprise!

Outside of sneaking away and being cultured on the best music I have ever heard in my life; I was a handful. I had a lot on my little mind as I started to gain independence and a sense of just who I was becoming.

Now, that didn't quite mix with my aunt and uncle and their rules, so bumping heads with one another was a daily, weekly, and monthly event.

This time in my life, I was doing my best to call my own shots. My friends were amazed at just how much I "got away with." They had no idea about the number of arguments that I would get into with my aunt and uncle during that time. In my mind, I'm sure I thought my life at that moment was temporary. I was not gonna always be under their roof. One day my mom was gonna return and I would be back home.

I can tell you that middle school breezed right past me. There were some good times and bad times, but mostly the times were filled with great music! I loved all kinds of music, but my love was Styx. Ohh buddy, they got me through a lot of mess.

Life was a little easier when I went to high school, because now I had friends who could drive.

I was never the perfect student or teen. I tested my teachers and my relatives. At that time, I was struggling with demons, and they had no idea how to help.

My anger had reached a pitch unlike they had ever seen, like we were speaking two different languages and they could not see just what I was going through. I had a crush mid sophomore year in high school, and he had become my refuge for the time being. It was rocky, also, but 2 outta 3 ain't bad. I loved that line in that song that really spoke to me,

I can't lie I can't tell you that I'm something I'm not, No matter how I try I'll never be able to give you something...something that I just haven't got.

MeatLoaf knew me, he knew that Fall of 78' was tearing me apart, tearing everything around me apart, and all I had to give was me. I couldn't be all that everyone else expected me to be. I was just being me.

If you know the song and really listen to the lyrics, it told my story in so many ways. As I always did, I substituted people, places, and things during my daydreams; this song just hit a little bit different. *Two Out Of Three Ain't Bad*

My family felt like I was gonna go down the same road as my mother, and they expressed to me that I would wind up just like her.

We could not get along. The counselor that I had at the time ended up removing me from my aunt and uncle's home and putting me in foster care. In hindsight, it was my fault. I was a handful and they were NOT equipped to deal with all that.

Eventually, my mother's rights were terminated and I became a ward of the State of Michigan. Once I was removed from my aunt and uncle's there was a "no contact" put into place. Several years went by when we did not communicate. Nothing unusual for me.

I was asked by the counselor how I felt. I said, "People come and go in my life – I'm used to it."

Chapter 9
"Foster Care"

I had a hole in my heart that nothing could patch. I struggled with my new reality and it started to sink in. I sat down and started to write this letter,

Dear Mom,

This is me, Lil Sheila,

I have been waiting on you to come back to pick me up,

You know I can't smile without you
I can't smile without you
I can't laugh and I can't sing
I'm finding it hard to do anything
You see I feel sad when you're sad
I feel glad when you're glad
If you only knew what I'm going through
I just can't smile without you
You came along just like a song
And brightened my day
Who would have believed that you were part of a dream
Now it all seems light years away
And now you know I can't smile without you
I can't smile without you
I can't laugh and I can't sing
I'm finding it hard to do anything
You see I feel sad when you're sad

I feel glad when you're glad
If you only knew what I'm going through
I just can't smile ....

Believe me, I really tried to write that letter, but all that I could do was remember this song that kept playing on the radio. I tried but I was in a Barry Manilow mood.

In the beginning, my first foster home was cool. The family had a son and a daughter my age. They lived in Dowagiac, so I just lived about three miles away from my aunt and uncle. I still attended Dowagiac schools. The State of Michigan paid this family to make sure I had clothes for school and to help with groceries and any medical needs.

My foster mother didn't like me much but my foster father did. I would go to work with him at the carwash and ride around with him in his big yellow truck. He was such a nice person. He treated me well and always told me that I would grow up to be a very important person, someday.

On the other hand, my foster mother was not as friendly. She took her daughter and me shopping in town at Wonderland and she bought both of us the same clothes; we had the same taste. It was almost like we were twins, with the same blue, silky tops, the same rhinestone watches, the same suede sweater coats.

When my time in their foster home was done, the mother kept all my clothes and gave them to her daughter. I did not take anything she'd bought for me when I left. I just went out with what I had when I came there.

Very strange situation. I kept in contact with her daughter over the years and we are still friends to this day. It wasn't her fault, so I had no animosity towards her, but I won't lie; just like her mom wasn't fond of me, I wasn't fond of her either! When my time was up there, it was on to the next foster home.

The next foster home was about 15 miles away, in Niles, MI. This time it was with only a new foster mother.

This woman wanted a maid. She had no interest in being a mom. She wanted someone to cook, clean and pick-up dog crap in the yard. She and I did not "click." It was a bad experience and once again it was very challenging. She worked from home and never left to go anywhere. Yard work and all cleaning and cooking were compliments of me. This woman had no business being in foster care.

A short time later, another foster girl was brought in. I liked Janet; we became friends and she was the only reason I was good with being there. Our foster mother used us to clean, scrub floors and toilets, and do everything around the house. Again, not much time was spent with us and helping us learn and grow. When I wasn't cleaning and scrubbing floors, I had a job.

I worked part-time as a dispatcher at the local township police department. There wasn't much crime going on in the Barron Lake area. I received calls about lost dogs or someone burning trash, and that was the extent of my 9-1-1 calls. To this day, I cannot remember how I actually got that part-time job. If I were to guess, I would say that my foster mother got me the job. The job was fun, but the best part was meeting people.

When I would get paid, I would have to give my money to my foster mom and she kept it, along with the money that the State of Michigan gave her for being in the foster care program. It was a win-win for this lady!

While working at the police station, I crossed paths with the township librarian. I confided in her a lot. She saw something in me that no one else did. We bonded and before I knew it, she talked to her husband and they took the classes required to become foster parents. So, when I was 15, they became my last set of foster parents.

This move was very important. They were the reason I became the only person in my family to graduate from high school. He was a teacher and she was a librarian, and they took time with me. They had two kids of their own, but they treated me well. They dealt with me and my antics. I tried to be a better kid but I won't lie, I still had trouble following the rules. I still felt like the "black sheep" but they truly took time with me. They wanted to see me succeed. The struggle was real but they never gave up.

Again, it wasn't smooth, but it was with them that I probably did the best. I met some great kids in school, I was a little more involved with things. They made it their mission to make sure I graduated and they helped me sign up for college grants and get ready for the step into adulthood.

They did their job, but once their job was done, they were ready for me to be on my way. The day I graduated from high school, I came home to find a bottle of champagne, a card with some cash in it, and a laundry basket filled with necessities for college, like towels, laundry soap, deodorant, dishes, etc., and they sent me on my way. No hard feelings, but I think they were done with fostering me and ready for me to start my next chapter.

I had a nice maroon 1979 Cougar with a plush grey interior. It was loaded, and good thing it was, because I lived in this car for three months! Anyone who remembers this car knows it was a boat, and man, it really sucked on gas!

Chapter 10
"Living Life on my Terms"

While living in my car that summer, I worked at a pizza chain in South Bend, IN, but shortly after I started there, they needed me to work in Valpo, IN. So, I would drive there to work, and sometimes sleep in my car and get cleaned up there in the morning. I couldn't afford the gas money to go back and forth from Valpo to Niles. I enjoyed this job; for the first time in my life, I started to feel as if I were going to be someone important, someday.

I was a seasoned vet with spending time to myself and by myself, so for the average person, sleeping in their car and being homeless would have felt like hell. All those days I spent in that apartment in Chicago, and later feeling alienated by my grandparents had taught me how to depend on myself and only myself. I looked at it as an adventure, you know, what creating forts with your sheets would feel like when you were a little kid.

During those times when I slept in my car, it gave me a whole new perspective on life. It was all summed up in one phrase: "You are all you got." I felt it, even more, when I would go out with my coworkers and they would say their goodbyes; they'd say they were heading home to shower and get some sleep, and they'd see me back at work the next day. They were going home to hot water, a cool bed, nice, crisp bed pillows and duvet comforters to cover their bodies, being awakened by alarm clocks or the smell of breakfast being made by their grandmother or mom. Imagine that... I could only...

As I drifted off into la-la land, tightly nestled in the backseat of my car, with the windows slightly cracked, I tried to get comfortable. I had traveled halfway to Niles that evening, and my body was too tired to make the full trip. I found an area to park right near a busy 24-hour gas station. Parked at the rear entrance of the parking lot, I made myself comfortable.

I fell into a deep sleep... My mind started to ramble, going over everything that I could remember since I was five years old, and I kept hearing a voice... "And it brought you here L'il one, and it brought you here L'il one, and it brought you here L'il one...

I struggled to open my eyes... I could see the silhouette of a woman in the distance. She started talking to me and I could not make out what she was saying; it had been at least a good 20 minutes and it just sounded like Charlie Brown speaking. I could tell it was someone I knew who loved me. I received four kisses from her on my cheek and the last one was on my forehead. She disappeared and I was in the presence of a crowd of people, again not saying a word, but they showed me love, I could just feel it. I woke out of my sleep in a cold sweat, just wet all over, thinking about what had just happened. I grabbed my beach towel to wipe my face and a stream of water splashed on my face. My car was soaked, it had rained in my car overnight as I slept with the windows cracked. I had to go into the gas station bathroom to use those towels to dry off. Funny thing is, I did not have another dream like that for the rest of the summer.

I only had to do this – work in two places and live in my car -- for a few months, and then it was time to go to Grand Rapids and move into the dorm.

I was going to attend college for business management, but unfortunately, all the freedom was a little too much for me. I only made it one semester. I went to school for only 90 days, then left college. It was a great experience but who was I kidding? I barely made it through high school, why did I think I was smart enough for college?

After dropping out of college I only had plans for working the pizza job, until one day an old flame made his presence in my life. We were high school crushes and he was around a lot of the time when I was going through my rebellious stages. I figured this was a chance meeting again because we had lost touch during those months.

I came back to town and was cruising with a friend when I saw him again. I recognized him right away; he had a certain walk and swagger about him. He was the quiet, jock type. We reconnected again and we both agreed that we missed each other and we wanted to continue our relationship and then... Boom! Surprise! I'm pregnant!

Yeah, this was another poor choice I made, but hey, you aren't going to tell me what to do! I'm in love! I later realized that I was in love with the idea of being in love.

Our honeymoon was cut short. He went off to the Army and was stationed in Germany and I gave birth here while living with his parents. Of course, I had no experience in raising a child. I knew nothing about "family" and they knew everything. No matter what I did, it was wrong. I didn't change him right, I didn't feed him right, I didn't burp him right.

Imagine being judged on everything that you do, and I could not just tell them, "Hey, I really don't know!"

For some strange reason, they thought that I did know what to do and criticized me about everything under the sun.

After a big-blow up, I ended up leaving with my little boy and going to a women's shelter. Again, no big deal. Been down this road before, I got this! Once again, alone and now it's *not* just me, I have a helpless baby who is depending on me, too.

I called for help for someone to take me in, but there was nobody. Finally, my last call was to my last foster parents and they agreed to give me a ride to Benton Harbor, MI to drop me off at this women's shelter.

The shelter was full but they made room in the attic for us. They threw down a mattress on the floor and that's where we stayed, in the hot attic. Just in case you didn't know, Michigan has cockroaches, too, and they are not afraid of heights. They found us in the attic! They didn't seem to be as big as the ones in Chicago when I was a little girl, but they still were creepy!

Filled with too much emotion, I finally cried. It had seemed a lifetime, taking loss, after loss, after loss, and it had all seemed to not get to me. But it did. I remembered thinking, *what am I going to do?*

We spent weeks at the shelter. Each day was always something different and new, dealing with other women with their own personal problems, and mine were just getting started.

I stayed up nights just thinking, *how did I get myself in this pickle, being pigheaded and a know it all.* I really was banking on love but it did not turn out the way I thought love would be. And how would it? I had said to myself, all those years as a little girl, that I would never get someone like Bill.

All that running in my mind and not listening to anyone, because Sheila knows best, I found out I didn't know that much.

My Bill was a carbon copy of my mom's Bill, not in color but in all actions; we never really got along. When he returned to the States, we got us a nice, old green trailer to live in and we attempted to play house. I think it was THEN that I realized why my mom gave up and sent me away. She knew she couldn't handle it and I had a better chance of making it elsewhere. I was now in a very similar situation as my mom. I had a controlling husband, a baby, and there was constant fighting.

I found myself spending a lot of time alone with my son and wishing that I could give him a better start in life and not repeat a cycle. I felt bad for myself, but I felt even worse for my mother, knowing just how it all felt. The desperation was just killing me.

I fell asleep after we had a knock-down, drag-out argument. Drifting off to music, as I always do, I could hear the voice in the background pleading with the shadow in the dark...

How can I just let you walk away...just let you leave without a trace...when I stand here taking every breath...with you...uhhh uh.... you're the only one who really knew me at all.... How can you just walk away from me, when all I can do is watch you leave...caus' we shared the laughter and the pain and even shared the tears.... you're the only one who really knew me at all.... so, take a look at me now.... cause there's just an empty space.... there's nothing left here to remind me, just the memory of your face.... take a look at me now.... there's just an empty space, and you coming back to me is against the odds and that's what I got to face.... I wish I could make you turn around.... turn around and see me cry... there's soo much I need to say to you, soo many reasons why.... Phil Collins knew my struggle.

I could see my mother in my dream and see myself in her place as the dream switched back and forth. I really could feel those words become flesh, as though they had been written just for me and this predicament I was in at that time.

I was a broken child and an incomplete adult, not really knowing what next move or action I needed to take in my life. I was at a total loss.

My husband and his family showed nothing but disdain for me; it wasn't totally my fault. He was Mr. Military barking orders at me 24/7 and that did not sit too well with me, so we were gonna have major problems. I had to look in the mirror and see what I had become: I had become my mother. I didn't have all the answers and I needed help.

We both agreed that divorce would be the best option for us. I ventured out into the world with my plus one and tried not to look back. My ex didn't want me to have our son, so he fought me tooth and nail for custody and he won full custody.

I had no other support system and he had his parents and his military background, so the cards were stacked against me. I was ordered to pay $22 a week in child support. He never enforced it, he just wanted control of our son. The funny part was, he didn't want custody. He just didn't want me to have him. Our son ended up living with his parents and they ended up raising him, not his dad or me. I was allowed to visit and take him to spend the night with me, but as he got older, he had other things he wanted to do than to come stay with me.

Eventually, I landed in a town a few miles away with a friend, the same friend, Janet, that I had met in an earlier foster home. She allowed me to stay there with her and her daughter. She basically took care of me. Gave me a roof over my head, food and stability, and our friendship was my saving grace of sorts. During time that I spent living with her, I learned a lot. She taught me how to make meatloaf with

90

Stove Top Stuffing. We ate corn and mac and cheese every other day. I watched her raise her daughter and, in some ways, raise me. I didn't know where I was going, but I was going there fast.

By now, I had a job at a hospital in a nearby town, Patient Registration, and I bought myself an orange Mustang. I was attempting to get to some type of "norm." I would see my son on the weekends and take him to the zoo and the park. Places that didn't cost much money.

Once again, I was trying to pick up what pieces were left of me and find the positive. I would tell myself; *this is a good thing that my ex-husband did this. He knew that I had no home and was just "crashing with a friend," and our son would be much better with him.* Or should I say, with *his* parents. He eventually moved to another town and got married, but he left our son with his parents. As time went on, more and more distance came between us. I would go months without seeing my boy, but don't get it twisted. He was always on my mind and in a locket that I wore close to my heart. Reality is, he was safe, well-provided for, and in a much better place than I could provide at that time.

Chapter 11
"Who is Sheila"

I learned early in life that expectations were the leading causes of disappointment. I think this all started with that damn Mr. Goodbar™ that I never got! They say when you learn to accept instead of expecting your life will be so much easier. There's some truth in that.

I don't think I ever expected much in life. I just wanted to feel important to someone and feel loved.

I accepted what crumbs people wanted to throw my way, but I won't lie, I wanted the whole cake with the buttercream frosting; it seemed to be hard to get that. Why couldn't I have my cake and eat it too? It goes deeper than that, I suppose, because we are all products of our environment and experiences and that's all we have to go on until we experience a little more and learn from it all.

Life was sure giving me a front-row seat, and just like in school, I felt like I was failing miserably. Janet was a very good friend to me and she helped me answer a lot of those questions in life. She would always say, "if you don't know yourself you will never know what you want or deserve." She had a point, and I looked at everything in a better way, listening to her. Because things could be worse, even still, things could be worse.

I started taking more time investing in what I liked about myself, who I really was, not what folks had told me, but just who Sheila really was. I concentrated on my likes and dislikes and worked on normal problem solving, where I could control my thoughts and emotions and just how I reacted to things.

I understood even more that my mother giving me to my grandparents was for the better, my son being with my ex-in-laws was for the better. I thought about what I could have given him at that time. I could barely take care of myself. So, I stopped being so combative and just stayed reflective and appreciative about what I did have. There was still a bit of me that left me cynical, because people may not want the best for me, just what they want for themselves.

The more I went out meeting new people and being exposed to the world and working on myself, I hit a place in my life where the hurt just came back full blast. No one told me how to deal with it, other than "Just deal with it." I wanted to make things right with my son's father and make it right with my son. Me not having total custody of him, not spending the "time with mommy" phase, hurt me to the core. I never gave up on love for my son and caring for him.... I would fall asleep humming, *Time after Time .... If you're lost you can look and you will find me...time after time...if you fall, I will catch you. I will be waiting...time after time...*" - Cindy Lauper

I started having that feeling again of being alone and no one actually caring about my feelings, so I became hardened for a while. Then, to add insult to injury, *Styx*, my favorite band, broke up; band members went on to do other solo projects but it just didn't feel right. I was in a sappy mood that whole year, you know, breaking up is hard to do. No matter if it's a good or a bad relationship, you have a part of them and they have a part of you. I remember crying my eyes out singing this song in the shower...

What can I do... pictures of you still make me cry...trying to live without your love...it's so hard to do...some nights I'll wake up...? I'll look at your pillow... hoping that I'll see you there......Don't let it end! Baby we could have so much more don't let it end... honey please don't; walk out that door..." Styx

*****

It's Summer 1985 and music videos and blockbuster movies are all the craze! *Legend, Back to the Future, Mad Max and the Thunder Dome, Rambo, The Breakfast Club, Cocoon,* and *Mask*. If you know the movie lineup you know it was a very emotional summer. I was learning who I was that summer and the sights and sounds around me took me

95

to another place. I could explore and be a conqueror like those in the movies, experience the hard reality of rejection, and hold on to the hope and dreams that one-day things would turn around.

I cried for a week-long after seeing the movie *Mask*, not because he had a deformity that was gonna later kill him, but because he had hopes to travel the world and it never happened for him. It was all that he had, the hopes, dreams and imagination. I saw myself just like many of the movie characters with hope, hope to love again, live again and get it right, but then the summer's anthems had me all over the place. I tell you '85' had me all over the place.

I was still trying to deal with giving my heart to my high school crush, having his child, not having my son with me full-time, and dealing with all of my life's baggage in general. Calling it an emotional roller coaster really did not do justice to the description of my life at that time, it just couldn't. I managed to survive the early 80's, keep in touch with my son, and work on myself, hoping that I was doing enough. I continued to work at the hospital, date a little, and just try to move on.

I was no longer cynical and saw life as it was, short and very promising, 'cause you just never know what's behind the next door.

Chapter 12
"Mr. Good Time Party Guy"

I met my second husband in the mid-80s while he was playing in a band and I worked in the hospital. My friend Janet introduced us. She had been following this band for a while and she wanted me to meet the lead singer.

We made plans to go to a local bar called the White House, also known as the Fight House. I had never been in this bar and was always led to believe it probably was a good thing I hadn't, because it was a little rowdy! But I agreed to go with her and meet this nice musician. We walked in the Fight House and there he was on stage in spandex, with fishnet nylons on his arms, handcuffs hanging off his waist, eyeliner, and long hair. He looked like Ozzy!

I told her, "NO WAY! Are you serious? This guy has no job, no car, and lives at home with his mom." He did sing in a band and he was a damn good singer, and to this day, I've never heard anyone sing *Barracuda*, by Heart, the way he did! But for the life of me, I could not figure out why Janet thought this guy was the guy for me. But she felt in her heart we belonged together.

It took eight months for him to get a date. We spent time getting to know each other; he would stop over to see Janet and hang out, and as time went by, one thing I noticed about him was his sense of humor. He was a conversationalist and always had something to say. I figured it had something to do with him being a musician, sometimes they would do original music or cover new and old music.

We had found our youth again, talking on the phone all night long, "You hang up, no you hang up..." we had found a teenage kind of love.

I hadn't had that type of fun in a long while but when we did, we connected, and before long, he got a job, got his car fixed, and we moved in with one another. Life was a big party. He was funny and I was living a rock and roll lifestyle.

I won't bore you with all the booze that was consumed and all the late-night fights at bars, but we had a good time. We were young, and let me say this, we never met a party we didn't like!

We lived together for five years before we married. Times were hard, money was tight, but LOVE, LOVE will keep us together. I think Captain and Tennille sang it best. *"We had good, bad, and ugly times, but we hung on..."*

Finally, in 1993 we had a son. I was ready for this; I was almost 30 years old and had been with my husband since 1985. We had a home and I thought, *I got this!*

We took a break from the bar scene for a few years and we both raised our son together. Again, the struggle was real. I had no idea how to raise a son. My first son still lived with my ex-in-laws. Even though we were married and attempting to raise a son, my husband had no father growing up, so together we were trying, the blind leading the blind.

I think we both felt like we wanted the best for our son and that backfired. I found myself in familiar territory again, trying to be a "friend" and not upset my son when I should have been a mother. My fear was, if I was too "mean" I would lose him too.

Life was happening, it had become a fast-paced life, and I had lost my reflective mind. I was now entering into full-blown adulthood and my ways of coping started to change, also. Mr. Goodbars™ weren't quite doing it for me anymore. I celebrated my victories with the same thing I celebrated my failures with, Jager, Crown, Hot Damn, and to be honest, any shot would do. I couldn't tell that I was drowning myself in over-indulging.

When our son got a little older, my husband got back in a band, we built a couple of homes, drove Hummers and life was good. Back in the bar scene on the weekends, the band table was reserved for 20 and our bar tabs were at about $350 a night. We spent more than the band got paid.

I was getting older and it took longer to recoup after being out till daybreak. My "check liver light" was coming on every weekend and I experienced alcohol poisoning not once but twice. I was slowing down. I was tired.

Our son got older and the typical challenges that come with a teen were now upon us. The stress of our son's choices made for arguments between me and my husband. We spent more time fighting over how to handle our son and I stopped going out to his gigs.

I think this was when we realized we were growing apart. He wanted to still be in the bar doing what he loved, and I had grown bored with it. I wanted to do more with my life than drink, dance, and continue to lose my hearing from loud music. I was spent.

For much of our marriage, I was the breadwinner. I always made more than he did but it didn't matter. We still put it in the same pot and made things happen.

Eventually, he got a good-paying job, made more than me, we built our second home, and we had things we hadn't had before. Life was boring and routine, but it was good.

I wanted to do more fundraising things and volunteer. He wanted to party. Twenty-seven years later, we called in quits. His plant closed down, he lost his job, and it snowballed from there. We lost our home we built five years earlier, filed bankruptcy, let the house go into foreclosure and decided to divorce.

We were moving but I had made up my mind we were moving onward separately. He didn't want the divorce but he knew if my mind was made up there was no changing it. We calmly talked and divided things up. He didn't fight me on it, but he was hurt and still to this day, he hates me. Hard to believe that you can spend that many years with someone and end up strangers. But we weren't the same people we were in our 20's. I was now 48 and in a totally different place.

He has remarried and moved on but we are not friends. As some divorced people tend to do, he only remembers the bad times. He forgets we had many great years and some awesome experiences and a handsome son out of it. It's ok and I know it was the right thing to do, because we were no longer living life. We were just existing and paying bills, and trying to keep things together for our son.

In 2012, after 27 years with my husband, it was done. Now what? This was a man that I had been with since 1985.

I had always had his leg to throw my leg over. I saved his life, not once but twice. We had a son, two dogs and so many friends; his family was my family.

Now what?

For the first time since I was young, I was all alone, like really alone by myself. The feeling overwhelmed me and emotions rushed in that I couldn't contain. As many people experience during a divorce, friends chose sides, his family no longer talked to me, our son was angry, and once again, I found myself in a familiar place.

I rented a duplex and took one of our dogs with me. A couple of friends helped me move and again, I was starting over. That first night, I had no bed and very little furniture. I slept on the floor with Coco and cried. This was a very familiar feeling that I had not had in so long. *But why am I crying?... this is what I wanted!*

I later realized I was crying because I missed the stability, I missed having someone there, I missed routine, and I missed what I had planned for my life. I told myself, *I will take this time to mourn the loss, but tomorrow will be a new day and I will get myself going in the right direction.*

Well, it took a little longer than 24 hours, but in three months I bought myself a brand-new car! It was my Valentine's Day gift to myself and this was my first Valentine's Day alone in a very long time. I treated myself good.

I continued to lose some weight and work on myself and what it was I wanted to do in this new chapter. For the most part, it went fine, not great, but fine.

I was successful at finding every whack job in the city, and once I conquered that city, I branched out to another city, where those whack jobs were at a totally different level. Oh, I had become a serial dater.

I wasn't ready for an intimate relationship but I did crave companionship, someone to do things with, someone to talk to about my day. I chose to go a year and a half without getting emotionally involved or having sex with anyone.

During this time, I met Mr. Player; Mr. Drunk; Mr. Druggie; Mr. Liar; Mr. Broke; Mr. Still Married but I act Like I'm Single; Mr. Partier; Mr. No Car, Pick me up for our Dates; Mr. Lazy; Mr. Narcissist; Mr. Controlling; and Mr. God's Gift to All Women.

I finally decided I had met the best of what was left out there for me, now in my 50's. He owned a business; he owned his home; he owned a couple of motorhomes; he was good at drag-racing; he had no kids; he had only been married once, and he was five years older than me. I'm thinking, *this has got to be it, right?*

Remember, one of the first things I said in this book was that you will cross paths with three types of people in your life? This fell under the "Reason" section. Let's just say I learned a lot from this relationship. We did not marry but I went against my better judgment and moved in with him. People say follow your heart, but take your brain with you. It appeared I left my brain at the train station.

I found myself in a very dark place. I truly lost all interest in going on in this world, if this was what it was going to be like the rest of my life.

I tried this for just over two years, and finally, I had reached the end. I needed to make a change, or I would have died of a broken spirit.

I was in such a dark place and was feeling as if I had failed again. *How did I end up here?* I had been so careful not to end up with the wrong person. I had lost my spark. This relationship taught me the most.

It was only a couple years, but it felt like 40 years. It was in this relationship that I learned I was stupid and should be ashamed to call myself a woman. I was in such a deep, dark hole that I wasn't sure I could crawl out of it. I also started the process of menopause during this time, so my emotions and weight were all over the map.

I could feel my heavy heart, my broken soul, and my confused brain just giving up. I was mentally exhausted and depressed at a level where I had never been. It was clear that this relationship was not working and I was definitely not for him, but how do I get out?

We may not be right for each other in a relationship but I wanted to remain friends. But why? Why was it important to me to still be his friend after he treated me the way he did?

With help from my boss and coworkers, I moved out. You see, it was this relationship that taught me to walk away: To walk away from arguments that lead to anger, from people who put you down, and from anyone who doesn't see your worth. I learned to walk away from mistakes and fears, because they didn't (and don't) determine my fate.

The more you walk away from the things that poison your soul, the healthier and happier you will be. Instantly, I felt the weight lifted off my shoulders (not off my butt, as I had put on 30 pounds during this relationship) It's done and it was one of the most educational experiences that I had ever been part of. I later realized we were not right for one another right out of the gate.

The problem was, he was trying to change for me, and he was also trying to change me for him. Neither one of us could be who we really were. In the end, I became somebody totally unrecognizable to those who knew me. I lost my humor, my spunk, my spark, my wit, and my confidence. I lost myself. When I left that relationship, I wasn't sure that I could boil water correctly, I was stir-crazy.

I had heard about this type of relationship in songs over the years but could never really understand how in the world it could happen to anyone. Love can be a strange thing, you will do any and everything for it, plus when someone has your number, you never know how you will act. So, yes, I was gone, on cloud 9, 10, 11, 12, and definitely 13. I had known, at a certain point in the relationship, that it was not serving me at all, and that it could be the death of me, but something in me did not want to give it up.

We had gotten to a point where the very things that brought us together -- trust, loyalty, a good heart -- were gonna be the death of us. We were too busy trying to make each other over that there was nothing left in my tank to give.

You know that old saying, "Love is blind?" I must've been triple-blind, because I could see but could not react to what I knew was bad for me; I just couldn't leave it alone.

For years I had lost my abilities to cope, dream, think and soothe. One day, I decided to turn to what was always my connection with my feelings, some music. It was always there during the times I needed it, but for some weird reason, it could not find me and I could not find it, remember life happened, and I was drowning.

I grabbed my phone, pressed play on my playlist I had downloaded a month prior, and then the song played...

Welcome to the Grand illusion
Come on in and see what's happening
Pay the price, get your tickets for the show
The stage is set, the band starts playing
Suddenly your heart is pounding
Wishing secretly you were a star
But don't be fooled by the radio
The TV or the magazines
They show you photographs of how your life should be
But they're just someone else's fantasy
So, if you think your life is complete confusion
Because you never win the game
Just remember that it's a grand illusion
And deep inside we're all the same
We're all the same
So, if you think your life is complete confusion
Because your neighbors got it made
Just remember that it's...

I took from that song that no one is perfect, we are constantly fighting against something or someone, and I had to get over it all, get over myself, and stop beating myself up from all of my past mistakes...life is what I make it.

*****

It's was now 2019. I'm starting over again. New apartment, new city, and I am now 54. It's not a new chapter. It's a totally new book. I have closed that book and burned it and spread the ashes over the lake. I'm still menopausal, and now borderline batshit crazy, but I got this!

I was just fine with being alone again. I was not looking and had no interest in looking. I think I was halfway considering becoming a nun. And then, he came along.

I tried to avoid him. I told him, "I'm not in a good place right now. I have issues. No, to be honest, I have the whole yearly subscription. I'm really not going to be a good fit for you. I need some time."

We went slow, and God bless his soul, he knew. He saw a spark in me and he saw something beyond my exterior looks. He saw my heart and soul, and in my eyes, he knew we were perfect for each other.

Not a day goes by that I don't thank him for taking that chance, thank him for his patience, for his understanding, and for the most important thing: For just being himself and allowing me to be me!

He is the most remarkable person that I have ever met, and I cannot imagine my life without him. He has helped me get my sense of humor back, he has calmed my soul and made my heart smile again. I feel safe and loved in a way that I have never felt. He is the reason I decided to write this book. He makes me want to be a better person.

He loves me 30 lbs. heavier or 30 lbs. lighter. He loves me when I struggle with my vices. He doesn't judge or criticize me. We work together as a team and this is the best feeling ever!

Remember those three types of people? Well, he falls in the "Lifetime" category. I have never met anyone like him and with him in my corner, there is nothing that I can't do.

2020 was a bad year for many reasons, but for me, I married my soulmate, we bought a home, saved a dog from the shelter and worked on being involved in our community and volunteering.

I am truly blessed and I have learned to let go of people who bring drama to my world. If you want to come in, the door is open; if you want to leave, the door is open, just do me one favor... Don't stand in the doorway, you're blocking traffic.

Chapter 13
"Motherly Love"

One thing that has kept me going all these years has been finding the good in every situation. For example, people have asked me:

"Aren't you mad at your mom for giving you up?"

"Aren't you mad that you don't know who your father is?"

My answer is, "No. I truly believe everything played out like it was supposed to. Had my mom not done what she did, I probably wouldn't be here. I'm sure I would have been dead a long time ago. So, I *need* to tell myself that she did what she had to do at that moment."

Unless we are in a situation, we cannot say what we would do. I can tell you, due to that choice she made, she saved my life. Still, without the love of a mother or father, I could not give that to my children.

I never really learned how to be a mother. I just don't have that "motherly instinct." I have a "survival instinct." I don't know if that came outright. Let me just say that I love my boys very much, but I am not good at showing it.

While I'm being so honest here, I am not a good mother. I blame no one for that except me. I'd like to blame my mom, my 3rd-grade teacher, or the Sunday school bus driver, but I just blame myself. I focused so much on not doing to my boys what was done to me that I was not their mother. I tried to be their "buddy," I wanted to be their friend.

I didn't want to whip them because I truly feared, if I started, I would not stop. So, in my mind, warped as it might be, I thought the "time out" approach was much better. Looking back, I'd say I probably should have done the spankings. I wanted the beating cycle and the abuse to STOP here, with me!

In the process, I failed at being a good mother. Any time I made the threat to whip my youngest, he would say, "You go ahead and whip me, and when I go to school tomorrow, I'm going to tell them you beat me and they will take me away."

Yeah, my youngest son won that one. I couldn't bear that thought. I always caved under pressure.

I've always worked and never took government assistance. I tried to show my boys that with hard work you can have good things. Yes, I told them to always stick up for themselves, but somewhere along the line, they heard, "Stick up for yourself and every one of your friends, and if someone hurts your family or friends, beat their butt!"

I expected more for my boys, so at times I thought money would help. Give, give, and give some more. Then they will LOVE me.

That too backfired! They had no respect for me. If I said no to them, that would make things worse between us.

I guess I made the error of expecting things to be different, when things were really no different than when I was growing up. My mom failed me, I failed them. We really don't understand each other. It is sad. I'm not proud of it, but it is the truth.

There was potential there, but sometimes you trip and fall over potential, hit your head on reality, and it can really hurt. How do you fix it so late in life? The damage is done.

You can put a band-aid on it, but it will never heal. You can soothe it with bullshit, but there will always be a deep scar.

If I can say one thing about expectations, it would be, "Life owes you nothing. It doesn't even promise you tomorrow. You were given life, but the pursuit of happiness is all up to you."

I think my mom expected a "how-to" manual when I was born, with "How to Raise your Newborn," but all she got was a package of cloth diapers, some diaper pins, and a can of formula. Again, it's that expectation thing. Bites you in the butt every time!

Chapter 14
"Choices"

You are totally entitled to make whatever choices you choose to make in this life. You will also be blessed with the consequences of those choices. Choose wisely!

That means, if we are given a crappy life, we have the choice to change it when we are old enough to do so, or we take it out on the world, blame everyone, and then go out and raise havoc. Some people shoot other people, rob banks, rape women, hurt kids, have sex with farm animals, or give hand jobs in back alleys for drugs or double cheeseburgers and use the excuse of a "bad life" for their actions.

Others choose to prove everyone around them wrong. For example, suppose in all your life you are told that you are ugly, that you won't amount to anything, that you will be just like your mother, and/or that you are a worthless piece of crap. What are your choices?

Now, you can cave, and say, "You're right. I'm going to go out and hurt others because I've been hurt all my life."

Or you can say, "Joke's on you! I am going to show you that I am somebody. I will be the first person in my family to graduate. I will go to college, (short-lived but I went). I will have a job and a car, even though I may have to live in my car, but this too shall pass. It might pass like a kidney stone, but it will pass."

And you can say, "I will show you that I got this. I will stumble and fall, but at no point will I fall down a flight of stairs and break my neck. You will be proud of me someday. It might be when I'm 40, 50, or 60, but I will make you proud."

Everyone processes things in a different way. Some people choose drugs, alcohol, sex, gambling, or food to help get them through. I am very lucky that drugs were never an option.

In the '80s and '90s, I did my fair share of drinking. Let's put it this way: I kept Crown Royal™, Jägermeister™, Hot Damn™, and Buttershots™ in business! But even I knew when enough was enough! By my later 40's I was done. I was spent!

I had reached a different level in my life where I wanted to put more focus on helping others and putting energy into other areas than partying with my musician husband and wild friends.

He wasn't done yet; he still had rock and roll in his blood and Captain Morgan's™ in his glass. I decided we were on different pages in this book of life, and I wanted out. As I said, we divorced after 27 years together. It was a good long run that included some great times.

You can choose to hang with the "chickens" and just walk around clucking, or you can choose to soar with the "eagles." Just remember, most "chickens" end up on someone's dinner table, but "eagles" are protected!

Chapter 15
"Reflections"

Yes, I've had some bad stuff thrown my way, but I never want to forget the good stuff. I've had people who believed in me and offered me jobs. Even though I didn't have the experience, they knew I had the drive and willingness to learn. They saw something in me, when I couldn't see it myself.

To many of you, this may seem average, but for me, it is incredible. For someone who didn't know where she would get her next meal, who would be taking care of me, or if I would even live to see my teens, I am proud!

I've met Oprah several times and have been on her show. I had a makeover done on the Sally Jessy Raphael Show. I wrote and appeared in a Hoosier Lottery Commercial. I was a part of many local "ribbon-cutting ceremonies" when I worked for the local government. I was a top salesperson when selling cars. I've received many awards for achievements. I've organized several fundraisers to help those in need, including the Humane Society.

I am far from perfect and I admit this in this book, but damn it, I made it through!

How did I do it? I'm not sure if it was with the help of the Man Upstairs, or if it was just pure determination to survive. I am not going to question it, I'm just going to continue to learn, grow, and help where I can, because I know what it's like to be the person living in their car, to have no gas money, and to have no food.

What I have learned is, people helped me from time to time, and I appreciated it and did what I could to make it right. I did not abuse their kindness.

When asked if my cup is half-full or half-empty, my only response is that I'm thankful I have a cup.

I've tried to repay and help others, but some people just used me. They took and took, to the point that they could no longer get blood, so then they gnawed at my bones.

It was never enough and I had to remove myself from those people, because I no longer could help them. They were not wanting to help themselves. Sometimes you have to remove toxic people from your space, family, or not. It is a poor choice on your part to mistake my kindness as a weakness – I am the furthest thing from weak!

"Toxic" and "drama" have no place in my world. For my sanity, I've had to remove myself from those people. I will go above and beyond to help someone, but if I see that they aren't putting forth the effort to help themselves, I will take my toys and leave them to play their games by themselves.

I feel sorry for those who don't have a sense of humor. Life is hard, and it's even harder if you can't find humor. My current husband will tell you, even in the most difficult situations, I always try to find the funny, or at least not dwell on the bad part but focus on the good. If you look hard enough, you will find something good in every situation. Even a broken clock shows the correct time twice a day.

I even use a sense of humor to explain why I don't miss my mom and dad. People have asked me, "Don't you miss them?" "Isn't it rough without them?" Again, using humor, I answer: "The best way to explain it is, it's like having a garage door with an automatic opener. If you never had one, you don't miss it. If you are used to getting out of your warm car and lifting the door up yourself, it's no big deal. However, if you have had an automatic garage door for 30 years, and every time you enter the driveway you push a button and it just goes up on its own, but now it is broken and you have to get out of your car in the rain and figure out why this door isn't going up... Yes, you are mad and miss that automatic door opener. But my mom and dad? I never had them to miss them."

I will add, "Now, if I had them until my 20's or 30's, and they passed away, then, yes, I am sure I would miss them terribly, but you can't miss something you never had."

It's like this: You can't make someone stay if they want to go. So, even though life has not been easy, and it's been like playing naked twister after six shots of Crown on a grease-covered vinyl twister mat, I'm still laughing and happy to be here. They say that sometimes you can be so damaged that when someone wants to give you what you truly deserve, you have no idea how to respond.

I have stopped swimming oceans for people who won't jump over a mud puddle for me. I'm 56 now. I still suffer from anxiety, I'm claustrophobic, I still rub my hands together when I'm nervous and I still have nightmares from time to time but, I find myself at a calm stage. Peace is more important than driving myself crazy trying to understand why something happened the way it did.

LET IT GO!

You know, they say it's always calm just before the storm, so maybe death is near. I don't know, but I'm finally at a place that I love.

I married the most incredible man on this planet this year, amid all this COVID stuff and negativity in the world. I married my best friend; someone I've known since high school. He keeps me grounded. He provides a good life for us. He accepts me and encourages me to be all I can be (You know like that Army slogan, "Be all you can be; join the Army.")

Anyway, all kidding aside, he has taught me things I should have learned years ago, but didn't. I am not going to complain about why I didn't learn or experience all this before, I'm just going to be grateful that I was able to marry this man and grow old with him and make the last years of my life the best ones yet.

As for my boys? They will be boys! They are now 36 and 26, and doing what makes them happy. I don't agree with their choices, but it's their life to experience. Do we have a close relationship? I have to be honest and say, no. I smiled when my oldest son would tell his friends that I'm the "coolest mom ever," but my heart breaks because he will never be able to say that I was the "best mom ever."

My youngest son doesn't understand why he is where he is. I try to explain that it's about choices. He just wants to say you can't keep bringing up the past; you have to focus on now. I tell him he's right, but he can't keep taking a left turn over, and over, and over, and over, and wonder why he keeps ending up at the same spot again and again.

I tell him, at some point he needs to make a right, go up over the bridge to the other side, look in the rear-view mirror for a moment, and keep traveling forward. But, again, my knowledge is boring to them and they know way more than I do. I understand that – as I was just like them at that age.

They both have kids of their own now and the cycle continues. I am not close with them, either. I really don't know how to be close with anyone. My husband is helping me with that, and together we are working on my insecurities.

In closing, please never let people dim your light just because it's shining in their eyes. Be kind; give them a pair of sunglasses.

I find it appropriate to end this book with a song. This is a country song that explains where things are at this point in my life. Even though it is a man singing about a woman, the words are also true for me and how thankful and grateful I am to:

"The Keeper of the Stars"
It was no accident me finding you
Someone had a hand in it
Long before we ever knew
Now I just can't believe you're in my life
Heaven's smilin' down on me
As I look at you tonight

I tip my hat to the keeper of the stars

He sure knew what he was doin'

When he joined these two hearts

I hold everything

When I hold you in my arms?

I've got all I'll ever need

Thanks to the keeper of the stars

Soft moonlight on your face oh how you shine

It takes my breath away

Just to look into your eyes

I know I don't deserve a treasure like you

There really are no words

To show my gratitude.

Sometimes music is the only medicine that the heart and soul

need.   -Tracy Byrd

THINGS I HAVE LEARNED:

Remember, there are 365 days in a year. Do a single act of kindness each day and you will have the ability to change 365 lives.

Never let anyone put out your fire. Even if it's just a spark, with just a small amount of fanning, it can become a flame.

To all the doors that closed on me, I'm coming back to buy the building and I'll have my people contact your people and we will do lunch.

We're all in the same game, just different levels. We're all dealing with the same hell, just different devils.

Don't forget: The dream is free! The hustle is sold separately!

Expectations are the leading cause of disappointment!

I was abused quietly, so I choose to heal loudly!

Life-changing events can live with you for a lifetime.

The heaviest burdens we carry are the thoughts in our heads.

Some people make things happen, some people watch things happen, while others wonder, "What the hell just happened?"

"Be so busy improving yourself that you have NO time to criticize others."

SONGS THAT WERE THE SOUNDTRACK OF MY LIFE:

1. *Christmas Carol* – Skip Ewing
2. *Wedding Bell Blues* – The Fifth Dimension
3. *Sittin' On The Dock Of The Bay* – Otis Redding
4. *Born to Be Wild* – Steppenwolf
5. *Lady* – Styx
6. *Two out of Three Ain't Bad* – MeatLoaf
7. *Can't Smile Without You* – Barry Manilow
8. *Against All Odds* – Phil Collins
9. *Time After Time* – Cindy Lauper
10. *Don't let it end* – Styx
11. *Grand Illusion* – Styx
12. *The Keeper of the Stars* – Tracy Byrd

C. Sparks is a native of Niles, MI, she is no stranger to struggle, hard times, and going without. Conquering every adversity that laid in her way, she defied the odds; yes, she still has flaws and faults just like the next human being but she never stopped trying to become a better version of herself. She believes that both victories and defeats have built her character and answered a lot of life's questions, with a resounding "Yes," she knew she could do it. You will feel all of the emotions known, and even learn a thing or two as C. Sparks brings you on the journey of her life with a musical backdrop that will, sure enough, spark grand memories. As Dick Clark put it, "Music is the Soundtrack to Our Lives," you best believe music helped C. Sparks keep it together and reflect during her whole life. This is not it by far! Look forward to more work from her this up-and-coming Year!

Made in USA - Kendallville, IN
1238624_9781949433166
02 24 2021 0809